☑ **W9-BCV-181**

CULTURES OF THE WORLD®
SRI LANKA

Nanda Pethiyagoda Wanasundera

BENCHMARK BOOKS

MARSHALL CAVENDISH
NEW YORK

PICTURE CREDITS
Cover photo: © Jeremy Horner/CORBIS
APA: 3 • Camera Press: 49, 52 • Charitha Gunawardena: 78 • CPA: title, 5 • Focus Team
Italy: 59, 84, 96, 102 • HBL Network: 35, 57 • Anthony Hughes: 42, 43 top, 44, 100 bottom
• The Hutchison Library: 110 • Image Solutions: 53, 114 • John R. Jones: 55, 60 • Life File
Photo Library: 3 bottom, 14, 25 top, 45 • Lonely Planet Images: 130, 131 • Dominic Sansoni:
3 top, 4, 7, 8 11, 12, 15, 16, 17, 19, 20, 22, 24, 25 bottom, 29, 32, 36 bottom, 38, 40, 41, 47,
62, 63, 64, 65, 66, 67, 68, 69, 70, 71, 73, 75, 76, 81, 82, 83, 85, 86, 87, 88, 89, 90, 91, 92, 93,
94, 95, 98, 99, 100 top, 101, 102, 103, 104, 107, 108, 109, 110, 112, 113, 114, 117, 119, 120,
121, 122, 124, 125, 126, 127, 128, 129 • Sri Lanka High Commission, Singapore: 13, 33, 36
top, 43 bottom, 46, 48, 51, 97 • Tan Chung Lee: 56 • Topham Picturepoint: 6, 31, 34, 106

PRECEDING PAGE
Children dressed up as nobility in Avissawella in Sri Lanka's Western province.

Marshall Cavendish
99 White Plains Road
Tarrytown, NY 10591
Website: www.marshallcavendish.com

© 1991 Times Editions Private Limited
© 2002 Times Media Private Limited
© 2004 Marshall Cavendish International (Asia) Private Limited
All rights reserved. First edition 1990. Second edition 2002.

® "Cultures of the World" is a registered trademark of Marshall Cavendish Corporation.

Published by Times Books International
An imprint of Marshall Cavendish International (Asia) Private Limited
A member of Times Publishing Limited
Times Centre, 1 New Industrial Road, Singapore 536196
Tel: (65) 6213 9288 Fax: (65) 6285 4871
Email: te@sg.marshallcavendish.com
Online bookstore: www.timesone.com.sg/te

Library of Congress Cataloging-in-Publication Data
Wanasundera, Nanda P. (Pethiyagoda), 1932–
    Sri Lanka / Nanda Pethiyagoda Wanasundera—2nd ed.
        p. cm.—(Cultures of the world)
    Summary: Describes the geography, history, government, economy, social life and
customs, religion, culture, and more of this island country in the Indian Ocean. Includes
a recipe for milk toffee.
    Includes bibliographical references and index.
    ISBN 0-7614-1477-0
    1. Sri Lanka—Juvenile literature. [1. Sri Lanka.] I. Title. II. Series.
DS489.W25 2002
954.93—dc212   2002025980

Printed by Times Offset Malaysia

7 6 5 4

CONTENTS

A Sinhalese child.

Fishing boats putting out
to sea.

Mother and child are illuminated by the glow of festival lamps.

INTRODUCTION

SRI LANKA, "RESPLENDENT ISLE," is a land of promise and potential, despite an ongoing civil war. An old name for the country, Serendip, inspired the English author Horace Walpole to coin the word "serendipity" and write a fairy tale called *The Three Princes of Serendip*, about three princes who keep making accidental discoveries during their travels.

Geographically, Sri Lanka is a speck in the Indian Ocean, just south of the Indian subcontinent. But this little island is big on attractions—natural, historical, and cultural. The coasts boast beautiful beaches and the forests contain unique plants and animals. The city of Ratnapura produces blue sapphires, cat's-eye, and other precious stones. Treasures from the island's past are found in the cities of Anuradhapura and Polonnaruwa and the rock fortress of Sigiriya. The civil war has left Sri Lanka's people with an abiding interest in politics.

GEOGRAPHY

ROUGHLY THE SHAPE OF A PEAR, Sri Lanka covers an area of 25,332 square miles (65,610 square km). The island measures 140 miles (225 km) at its widest and 270 miles (435 km) from Point Pedro in the north to Dondra Head in the south.

Sri Lanka lies just 30 miles (48 km) south of India, with which it shares the same continental shelf. Romantics call Sri Lanka the "Teardrop of India." To the island's south is the vast Indian Ocean, and to the east is the Bay of Bengal. In distant years past, Sri Lanka's position was strategically important, located on the major sea routes that linked Asia with Europe, the Middle East, and Africa.

Opposite: **The Sri Lankan coast is made up largely of rocky cliffs and sandy beaches.**

Below: **An ox gets a break from ploughing in a muddy stream.**

Overleaf: **Victoria Dam. Sri Lanka's waterways were used for irrigation as early as 2,000 years ago.**

PARADISE BORN OF UPHEAVALS

Geologists believe that Sri Lanka once lay beneath the sea. A series of earthquakes probably thrust the land up, producing an island with south-central hills crowned with mountains that slope sharply into valleys. Plains stretch out in the north toward the Jaffna Peninsula.

Sri Lanka's highest point is a mountain near the town of Nuwara Eliya. Pidurutalagala stands at 8,281 feet (2,524 m).

RIVERS, FALLS, AND TANKS

Most of Sri Lanka's rivers begin in the south-central hills and flow outward to the sea, tumbling over rocky precipices on the way and forming waterfalls.

Sri Lanka's longest river is Mahaweli Ganga at 208 miles (335 km), and its shortest is Gal Oya at 67 miles (108 km). The island's most famous waterfalls are the Dunhinda and the Diyaluma. The latter gets its name from the Sinhala word *diyahaluma* ("DI-yah-loo-meh"), which means "spilling waters." Sri Lanka's highest waterfall is the Bambarakanda, with a fall of 865 feet (264 m).

The rivers of Sri Lanka were tamed by the Sinhalese kings. Through feats of hydraulic engineering, the kings created artificial lakes and turned arid scrubland into fertile fields, earning Sri Lanka the title "Granary of the East." Some of Sri Lanka's man-made lakes, called tanks, date from the Anuradhapura period over 2,000 years ago. The government's most recent hydroelectric project was the Mahaweli Diversion Project. Construction began in the 1980s and was completed in five years.

LEGENDS OF THE FALLS

Sri Lanka's grand waterfalls have inspired poets, painters, musicians, and storytellers. Here are a few of the island's waterfalls:

The turbulent waters of the **Dunhinda** plunge from a height of 200 feet (61 m) into a large deep pool, where legend says a beautiful fish wearing a golden earring swims. The story says the fish swims over the buried treasure of Kumarasinghe, the prince of Uva, and comes to the surface only once a year. Legend also has it that the treasure is guarded by men armed with gold swords. Those who swim in the pool must beware, as the guardians of the treasure look for a human sacrifice every year.

A romantic legend associated with the Dunhinda tells of a princess from the Gampola Dynasty who eloped with her commoner lover. The unfortunate couple was tracked down to a village near the falls. Determined not to be separated, the couple fled to the highest ledge of the Dunhinda and jumped to their death. The same night, a terrible storm wiped out the surrounding villages. Even today, people say that they still hear the lovers' shrieks when storms reach their peak.

Lover's Leap in Nuwara Eliya has its source in the Pidurutalagala mountain. This waterfall is believed to be haunted by the ghosts of another runaway couple; they jumped to avoid an angry father.

The **Ravana** near Ella is named after the villain of the Ramayana epic. According to legend, the evil king Ravana once lived in a cave near this waterfall.

Bridal Falls is the name given to Saint Clair Falls in Talawakele, because its waters resemble a bride's veil.

Baker's Falls is named after its discoverer, Sir Samuel Baker, the British explorer who mapped the upper Nile. At Nuwara Eliya, Baker set up an experimental farm, where he introduced English vegetables.

Opposite: **Tree ferns of Nuwara Eliya, a town in the central hills.**

CLIMATE

Sri Lanka has a tropical climate. It is hot and wet through most of the year. Humidity is high in some places, making the daytime unpleasant, though nights are relatively cooler. Temperatures in the coastal regions range between 80°F and 83°F (27°C and 28°C). Temperatures in the northwest of the island can reach 100°F (38°C) and higher, while in the south-central hill country, the temperature hovers around 50°F (10°C). The hottest months are March and April, while the driest month is February. From December to January, the entire island enjoys a break from the tropical heat, and the hill country experiences an almost temperate climate.

Rainfall in Sri Lanka varies considerably from one region to the next. The central highlands receive the most rainfall, especially on the western slopes, where annual measurements of more than 200 inches (500 cm) have been recorded. The eastern slopes receive significantly less rain—under 138 inches (350 cm) annually.

The northwestern and southeastern lowlands receive the least rain. Rainfall in the north averages 40 inches (100 cm) annually, and up to 200 inches (500 cm) of rain falls in the southwestern mountains. The average rainfall is about 200 inches (508 cm) in the south-central hills and 75 inches (191 cm) in the north and east of the island.

There are two monsoon seasons each year. The southwest monsoon, active from May through September, is the main rain-giver. It waters Sri Lanka's wet zone, which includes the western, southern, and central hills facing the moisture-laden southwesterly winds. After shedding its moisture, the dried-out winds blow across the eastern plains. The northeast monsoon waters the northern and eastern parts of the country from December through March. It brings less rain than the southwest monsoon, though it can sometimes cause floods.

EVERYTHING IS GREEN

A visitor's first impression of Sri Lanka likely includes how green the island is. Trees in varied shades of green abound, and against the fresh green of leaves blazes the brilliant crimson of bougainvillea and flame-of-the-forest flowers.

Sri Lankan flora ranges from the mangroves on the coast and the dense tropical evergreen rain forest of the lowland wet zone to the thorny trees of the dry zone and the tough grasslands called *patana* ("PAH-teh-neh"), dotted with red rhododendron.

The primeval Sinharajah forest, with its tall trees and thick undergrowth, is home to the fast disappearing Vesak orchid and is now a protected area. Much land has been given to agriculture and forestry, and deforestation has left a clear mark on Sri Lankan soil.

"*Ordering by the beat of the drum that no animals should be killed within a radius of seven gau from the city, he gave security to animals. He also gave security to the fish in the 12 great tanks, and bestowing (on the people) gold and cloth and whatever kind of wealth they wished, he commanded them not to catch birds and so gave security to the birds …*"

—12th-century decree of King Kirthi Nissanka Malla of Polonnaruwa, engraved on a stone slab.

ANIMAL LIFE

Sri Lanka is well-known for its bountiful wildlife, although extensive land cultivation has forced many animals to retreat to the confines of the few remaining forests on the island.

Mammals living in the safety of the national parks include the Asian elephant, spotted leopard, sloth bear, black-faced langur, reddish-brown macaque, purple-faced leaf monkey, elk, barking deer, spotted deer, and mouse deer. Reptiles include the saltwater crocodile, leatherback turtle, iguana, and several species of snake, including the deadly cobra and saw-scaled viper. Most of Sri Lanka's fish live in the inland marshes and rivers. Rainbow and brown trout swim in the cold waters of the Horton Plains.

Above: **A protected monkey in Sri Lanka.**

Opposite: **Elephant and trainer cool off in the tropical heat.**

More than 400 species of indigenous and migrant birds have been sighted in Sri Lanka. Among the endemic species are the Ceylon blue magpie, Layard's parakeet, and chestnut-backed owlet. There are also barbets, flycatchers, and thrushes. In the Ruhuna (popularly called Yala) National Park, the peacock performs its mating dance in the months from December to May. Ruhuna—a semi-arid, thorny scrub forest in the southeast—is the country's largest national park after Wilpattu—a lush, thick secondary forest in the northwest. In 1985 the Liberation Tigers of Tamil Eelam (LTTE), a terrorist group, infiltrated Wilpattu, and the Department of Wildlife Conservation ordered the park closed to visitors.

Three other national parks in Sri Lanka are the Gal Oya, Uda Walawe, and Lahugala. At the Lahugala Tank in Lahugala National Park, elephant grass grows wild. Herds of wild elephants are drawn to this sanctuary during their migration through the island.

CITIES

COLOMBO Sri Lanka's capital lies on the western coast. The harbor bustles with merchant and cargo vessels, and the international airport at Katunayake is just 30 minutes away. The Galle Face Green promenade has many large hotels, the most famous being the over-150-years-old Galle Face Hotel. Colombo has a population of over a million and is divided into 15 postal districts. Slums sit alongside five-star hotels and palatial private residences. The center of the city and its commercial hub is the Fort, a Dutch fortification and the site of the president's residence. The Fort has been under tight security since an LTTE bomb attack on the Central Bank in 1996. A few miles east of Colombo lies Kotte, the ancient royal capital, where the new parliamentary complex stands in the Diyawanne Oya at Sri Jayewardenepura.

KANDY Cooler and more beautiful than Colombo, Kandy is no less congested. The tooth relic of the Buddha is preserved here, making Kandy an important place of pilgrimage for Buddhists.

JAFFNA Most Sri Lankan Tamils have their roots in Jaffna, the major battle ground of the LTTE. Desiring a separate state for Tamils, the LTTE started a civil war in Jaffna and ruled the peninsula before government forces regained control in 1996. The road through the Wanni region, the stronghold of the LTTE, is dangerous. Tamils going home to see their relatives travel by air or sea. Tourists visit Jaffna with military escort.

GALLE AND TRINCOMALEE Galle on the southwestern coast and Trincomalee to the northeast are natural harbors. Both have Dutch fortresses and a quaint, sleepy air. Trincomalee is the site of a major historical attraction, Swami Rock. The ruins of a Hindu temple sit squarely on a cliff that drops into the deep blue sea. Closenburg in Galle is a swimmer's paradise.

NUWARA ELIYA Nestled in the hill country, Nuwara Eliya is the gem of Sri Lanka's hill resorts. Remnants of British colonial influence are still seen in the colonial buildings and gardens. Nur'Eliya, as it is locally known, is also famous for its tea plantations.

Historically, Trincomalee was Sri Lanka's battleground, the scene of bitter fights between the Portuguese and the Dutch, and later between the Dutch and the British. Rising from the sea is Swami Rock, and on it the ruins of the Temple of a Thousand Columns, which was destroyed by the Portuguese in 1622. On January 23 each year, Hindus make a pilgrimage here with offerings at sunset. A beautiful legend is attached to this place, of a prince who pined for his princess and was turned into a lotus flower by the gods.

INLAND TRAVEL

Railroads connect Sri Lanka's cities. The trains are clean, reliable, and not overcrowded. Intercity vans and minibuses, on the other hand, are always jam-packed, with passengers hanging precariously out the doors.

Barges and outrigger canoes called catamarans navigate the canals radiating from Colombo. For those in no hurry, a cart drawn by an ox or a team of oxen ambles along, speeding up only when goaded by a sharp jab of the carter's stick. Mercifully, the rickshaw with its human beast of burden is no longer a mode of transportation.

Road travel in the towns and suburbs is a noisy, often hair-raising, experience. Carefree cyclists, motorbike maniacs, horn-tooting motorists, overloaded buses, and nonchalant jaywalkers contribute to the general mayhem.

In the less populated and more remote rural areas, however, newly paved roads offer a smooth ride, and even the older roads riddled with ruts, humps, and potholes are easy to travel, since they are comparatively free of traffic.

ADAM'S PEAK

Sri Pada, or Adam's Peak, is a conical rock rising 7,360 feet (2,243 m) in the south-central hills. On clear days, Adam's Peak can be seen even from Colombo on the western coast. At night, from December through March, Adam's Peak is visible from miles away, a string of lights reaching toward to the sky. The lights mark a steep path up the mountain slope.

Christians, Muslims, Buddhists, and Hindus venerate Adam's Peak. On the summit is a mark in the rock the shape of a giant footprint. Muslims say it is Adam's footprint, which he left there when God banished him from Eden; hence the name Adam's Peak. Christians believe it is the footprint of Saint Thomas, the apostle who brought Christianity to Sri Lanka. Buddhists believe the Buddha left his footprint on the summit during his final visit to Sri Lanka. And Hindus say the footprint is the god Shiva's. Further enhancing its religious role are the structures on Adam's Peak: a *dagoba* ("DAH-go-beh"), or Buddhist temple, a shrine, and a temple to the god Saman.

The most popular route for pilgrims and tourists climbing to the summit is a 2-mile (3-km) climb through tea estates and rocky terrain, followed by another 2-mile trek up sheer rock-hewn steps. On the way, the trekker passes a Japanese peace shrine (stopping to discard a needle and a ball of thread for luck), souvenir stands, and restrooms. Even water is sold, the price escalating as one's climbing stamina decreases!

Most people climb through the night in order to reach the summit at dawn—in time for the spectacular sunrise that throws the shadow of the peak for miles beyond. The amazing thing is that the pinnacle can accommodate so many people. A bell tolls continuously as pilgrims register the number of times they have climbed Adam's Peak by giving the bell-rope the corresponding number of tugs.

HISTORY

Opposite: The 39-foot (12-m) standing Buddha at the Aukana Temple is 1,500 years old.

MYTH AND LEGEND are woven into Sri Lanka's history, which spans 25 centuries. The *Mahavamsa* ("MAH-hah-VUM-seh"), a chronicle dating back to the sixth century A.D., and its sequel, the *Culavamsa* ("CHOO-lah-VUM-seh"), relate Sri Lanka's early history.

According to the *Mahavamsa*, before the sixth century B.C. there existed two tribes, the Yaka and Naga. Stone objects have been found that indicate *homo sapiens* probably lived in Sri Lanka around 500,000 B.C. From 5,000 B.C. until about 500 B.C., a people called Balangoda practiced stone-working technology. They dwindled with the arrival of the first settlers from India.

THE SINHALESE ARRIVE

The first royal dynasty was started by Prince Vijaya (543–505 B.C.). This Indian prince was banished from his father's North Indian kingdom because of his bullying ways. His father, Sinhabahu, was believed to be the offspring of a lion, or *sinha* ("SING-hah"), and a princess; hence the name Sinha, or Sinhalese, for Vijaya's descendants in Sri Lanka.

Vijaya arrived on the northeastern coast of Sri Lanka. Legend tells that a witch, Kuveni, fell in love with him. Abandoning her people, she gave up her realm to the newcomer, but after they had two children, Vijaya decided to start a blue-blooded dynasty. He ordered Kuveni and their children into the wilderness and married a South Indian princess. His dynastic dreams, however, did not come true. It was a nephew arriving later who established the Sinhalese community in Sri Lanka.

While Kuveni was slain by her people, her two children by Vijaya survived and are believed to be the ancestors of the aboriginal dwellers of Sri Lanka, the Veddhas.

The ruins of Anuradhapura, once the center of Sinhalese power and culture. This ancient capital is one of Buddhism's sacred cities. Among the historical treasures here is the Thuparama, which enshrines the sacred relics of the Buddha. The bodhi tree, grown from a sapling of the original tree under which the Buddha attained Enlightenment, is also located here.

BUDDHIST FOUNDATIONS

Culturally and spiritually, Sri Lanka is indebted to India. Buddhism was brought to the island by Mahinda, son of the great Mauryan emperor Asoka in the third century B.C. This was during the reign of Devanampiya Tissa, whose capital was at Anuradhapura.

When Buddhism became the state religion of Sri Lanka and the foundation of Sinhalese civilization, the country's classical era began. During this period, between 200 B.C. and A.D. 1200, art, architecture, and stone sculpture flourished. Huge temples were built to house relics of the Buddha. These temples are venerated even today and never fail to inspire the beholder with their simple form, peaceful appearance, and majestic size.

Sri Lanka's ancient civilization emerged in the island's dry zone—the extensive north-central plains and a smaller area in the southeast. The legacy of this ancient past lives on in the exquisitely carved statues, temples, reservoirs, and channels in these areas. An ingenious tank covering 7 square miles (18 square km) was built by King Mahasena (A.D. 274–302). Some 200 years later, King Datusena (A.D. 460–478) built the Kalawewa (*wewa*, pronounced "WAI-weh," means "tank"), a reservoir covering 7 square miles with a dam 36–58 feet (11–18 m) high and stretching 3 miles (5 km).

ANURADHAPURA: SEAT OF KINGS

Founded in the sixth century B.C., Anuradhapura is one of Sri Lanka's major historical sites. Once the seat of kings, Anuradhapura was the first capital of Sri Lanka. The city reached the height of power in the ninth century A.D., but was later displaced by Polonnaruwa.

In the second century B.C., Anuradhapura was the capital from which a just Tamil king named Elara ruled northern Sri Lanka. Ruhuna, the southeastern part of the island, was ruled by a Sinhalese king named Kakavan Tissa, and the southwestern region was the domain of King Kelani Tissa.

After Kelani Tissa killed a Buddhist monk, his daughter, Viharamaha Devi, was sent out to sea in a boat as a sacrifice. But winds blew the boat to a port in Ruhuna. There, Kakavan Tissa married the princess and they had two sons. The elder son, Gamini, raised an army to fight Elara. He killed Elara and became known as Dutu Gemunu, or Fearless Gamini. From Anuradhapura, he ruled a now-unified country that grew in prosperity. Dutu Gemunu built many temples, the most famous being the Ruwanvelisaya, which is surrounded by a wall of stone elephants.

"In the midst of this twined, entrenched woodland ... we came to the abandoned kingdoms of Anuradhapura and Polonnaruwa, capitals of the first Sinhalese kings. Their temples had been burst open by vines, trees grew through their thick walls. Hidden in a clearing ... an immense fractured Buddha lay on his side, sealed eyes calm ... to see these fallen monuments, invaded by the jungle, inhabited by beasts, made me aware of history."

—Dom Moraes,
Indian poet

Below: **Sigiriya Rock.**

Opposite top: **The reclining Buddha of Polonnaruwa.**

Opposite bottom: **A fresco at Sigiriya.**

SIGIRIYA

A violent king, yet one dear to Sri Lankans, is Kasyapa, eldest son of King Datusena of Anuradhapura. Kasyapa was afraid his half-brother, Mogallan, would inherit the throne. So he killed his father by walling him into a corner of the Kalawewa, the tank Datusena had built. Seizing the throne, Kasyapa built a palace fortress on Sigiriya, a tall plateau-like rock, to protect himself from the wrath of the rightful heir. Kasyapa ruled from Sigiriya for 18 years, from A.D. 477–95. Then Mogallan attacked, and Kasyapa killed himself, mistakenly thinking he had no defense.

Halfway up Sigiriya's sheer rock face are wonderful frescoes, paintings of beautiful women, some holding lotus flowers. Beside the rock-hewn steps winding up to the palace fortress is a remarkable lime-coated wall with a mirrored surface to protect the climber moving along the steps. Sigiriya's mirrored wall carries graffiti written by visitors who praise or ridicule the bare-bosomed beauties in the frescoes.

POLONNARUWA

The capital of the kingdom was moved from Anuradhapura to Polonnaruwa in the 12th century. King Parakrama Bahu I (A.D. 1153–56), a Sinhalese king, managed to gain control of nearly the entire island. During his short reign, several Buddhist shrines and monuments were added to Polonnaruwa. King Parakrama Bahu I is best remembered for the tank he constructed, called Parakrama Samudra (meaning "Sea of Parakrama"), of which he said, "Let not a drop of water flow into the sea before it is used in the service of man."

THE KANDYAN KINGDOM

With the decline of the classical age, the capital was moved several times, until the last kings located their capital in Kandy. This remained the capital until 1815, when the British colonial era began.

THE MANY NAMES OF SRI LANKA

Centuries before the birth of Christ, the island now known as Sri Lanka was called Thambapanni. In the *Mahavamsa*, it is written that "When those who were commanded by Vijaya landed from their ship, they wearied, resting their hands on the ground. And since their hands were reddened by touching the dust of the red earth, that region and also the island was named Thambapanni (copper-colored earth)."

When the Greeks and Romans visited the island, they adjusted the island's name a little, and Thambapanni became Taprobane, a name mentioned in several Greco-Roman texts. Ptolemy's second-century map of the island, captioned *Tabyla Asia XII*, uses this name for the island he traced. The ancient Sinhalese called their homeland Heladiva (Sinhadvipa in Sanskrit, Siholadipa in Pali). Heladiva was one of the richest places in Asia, located on the main trade route linking the Middle East with Southeast Asia and China (*below*). Arab traders called Heladiva Serendip. Horace Walpole coined the English word "serendipity" from this name.

The first Europeans who came as traders but stayed on as rulers were the Portuguese. They colonized the spice island in the early 16th century and called it Ceiloa. The Dutch wrested trading rights and colonized the island in the mid-17th century, changing the name to Ceylan or Zeiland. The British, who conquered the island and added it as another jewel to the British crown in the early 19th century, changed the name to Ceylon. This was the name the island went by even after independence from the British. In 1972, when the country assumed the status of a republic, it became Sri Lanka, which means "resplendent isle."

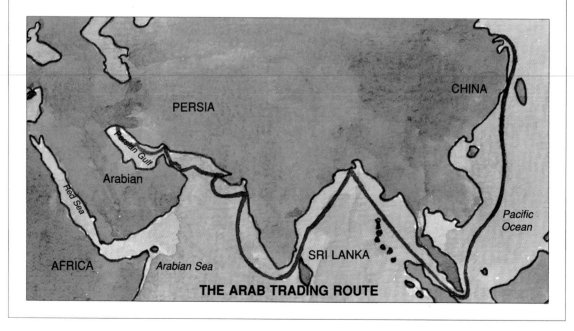

THE ARAB TRADING ROUTE

EUROPEAN COLONIZATION

THE PORTUGUESE The first Portuguese visit was "serendipitous." In A.D. 1505, a fleet commanded by Lourenco de Almeida was blown into the Colombo harbor and given a friendly reception by the Sinhalese king of Kotte. Impressed by the island's commercial and strategic value, the Portuguese landed in force in 1518. They were permitted to build a fort in Colombo and were given trading concessions. Soon they expanded their influence and turned from trading to ruling.

With intense zeal, Portuguese missionaries converted the indigenous people and forbade Buddhism. They lacked understanding of traditional Sinhalese society and were cruel in their demands. It is no wonder that when the Dutch appeared on the horizon as traders, the Sinhalese welcomed them as liberators and collaborators.

"There is in our harbor of Colombo, a race of people, fair of skin and comely withal. They don jackets of iron and hats of iron, they rest not a minute in one place, they walk here and there. … Their cannon balls fly many a gawwa and shatter fortresses of granite."

—S. Udugama,
Sri Lanka from Legend and History

"LIKE THE PORTUGUESE WHO WENT TO KOTTE…"

Kotte was the seat of kings from the mid-14th to the 16th century. The Sinhalese expression "Like the Portuguese who went to Kotte" describes how the first Portuguese envoy was led by a circuitous route from Colombo to Kotte so he would not realize that Kotte was only 5 miles (8 km) away. The ploy worked.

A few years later, a second Portuguese envoy, General Payoe de Souza, arrived and met King Parakrama Bahu VIII (*right*). His visit had a different ending. By 1557 the Portuguese had allied themselves to the next Kotte king, then killed him; baptized another Sri Lankan king and moved him to Colombo; and finally destroyed Kotte.

THE DUTCH In a period of intrigue and shifting alliances in the Dutch-Portuguese-Sinhalese triangle, local kings and lesser officials brought their influence to bear on the situation. By 1658 the Dutch had seized the Portuguese fort in Colombo and taken hold of their last strongholds—Mannar and Jaffna in the north.

Although the Dutch East India Company was first set up in the coastal regions, its influence eventually spread inland. But the Kandyan kingdom remained intact in the central hills and eastern province.

The Dutch left a legacy in Sri Lanka in the form of printing technology, the judicial system of Roman-Dutch law, and canals radiating from Colombo. Some of these canals are still navigable by boat and one leads the tourist to a bird sanctuary.

THE BRITISH The British East India Company was established in Sri Lanka around 1796. Contacting the king of Kandy, the British offered to replace the Dutch as protectors of the kingdom. The Kandyans were suspicious. In typical colonizing style, the British decided to unify the island under their rule. Sensing disunity in the Kandyan court, the British promoted treason. They eventually captured the king of Kandy and deported him to South India. By 1815, the British ruled the entire island.

The British introduced coffee in Sri Lanka as a cash crop. Coffee did very well from 1830–70, replacing the former main export crop, cinnamon. In 1870, however, disease destroyed coffee plantations in Sri Lanka. Tea and rubber replaced coffee and became better cash-earners.

Together with cash crops, the British introduced cheap labor from South India. Initially, South Indian Tamils working on coffee plantations would return to India after the harvests. However, tea and rubber required year-round care, so Tamil laborers began to settle in Sri Lanka, forming a

new group of Sri Lankan Tamils—Indian Tamils, who were distinct from the long-established Jaffna Tamils.

The British built roads and railroads in Sri Lanka and developed trade and commerce in both urban and plantation areas. The villagers, however, were mostly neglected. Their lands were purchased for a small sum to extend the tea estates, and they survived by growing food on whatever land they could find.

The British ruled Sri Lanka from 1815 to 1948. A governor-general in Colombo, government agents, and other officials administered the nine provinces into which the island was divided.

The Viceroy Special chugs through the lush green countryside, reminding Sri Lankans of the island's colonial past.

NATIONALISM AND INDEPENDENCE

From the late 19th century, a growing national political conciousness in Sri Lanka created a call for constitutional reform and self-government. While independence was still a long way off, in 1931 the British gave the vote to Sri Lankan men and women over 21 years old. (This was certainly progress; in Britain, women were given the vote only in 1929.)

When World War II broke out, Sri Lankan leaders suspended their nationalistic struggles and pledged support for the war effort. Trincomalee and Colombo became important link ports for Allied warships. A couple of Japanese war planes arrived on Easter Sunday in 1942, probably to study the terrain and plan an attack. They were repulsed.

Ceylon was the headquarters of the South East Asia Command (SEAC) under the charismatic Lord Louis Mountbatten, the last Viceroy of India and later the favorite uncle of Prince Charles. Trincomalee in northeastern Ceylon was an important habor for the Allied navy.

In 1945 Sri Lankans resumed their agitation for independence. Although they were granted internal self-government, with the British retaining control of defense and foreign policy, nothing short of independence would satisfy them. At last, the Ceylon Independence Act of 1947 conferred dominion status on the country. A year later, on February 4, Sri Lanka celebrated its independence from colonial rule with fireworks, feasting, and jubilation.

SHIFTS OF POWER

In the years before and right after independence, the spirit of nationalism ran high. Everyone was first Sri Lankan, then Sinhalese, Tamil, Muslim, or Burgher. But trouble soon followed, leading to the election of six governments in less than 35 years. Even today, Sri Lankan politics is irretrievably tied to economic troubles and ethnic tension.

Don Stephen Senanayake was Sri Lanka's first prime minister. The failure of his United National Party (UNP) to maintain a strong economy led to its downfall. In 1956 a new opposition party, the Sri Lanka Freedom Party (SLFP), led by S.W.R.D. Bandaranaike and backed by Buddhist leaders, won the national election. However, the party was divided on many issues, and tensions led to the prime minister's assassination in 1959.

THE FATHER OF THE NATION

Along with other national leaders of Sinhalese, Tamil, Muslim, and Burgher heritage, Don Stephen Senanayake (*right*), affectionately called the Father of the Nation, led the constitutional reform movement that gave Sri Lanka independence from the British.

Serving as the minister of agriculture and lands (1931–47), Senanayake engineered the rebirth of irrigation development in the country's dry zone. As Sri Lanka's first prime minister (1947–52), with Lord Soulbury as governor-general, Senanayake's moderate policies steered the country along the path of nation rebuilding. His special area of interest was self-sufficiency in food production.

Senanayake died in 1952 when his United National Party was still in power. His son Dudley succeeded him as Sri Lanka's prime minister.

The UNP took over the following year, but it was so weak that elections were held again just four months later. Sirimavo Bandaranaike, the assassinated prime minister's widow, led the SLFP to victory. She addressed the country's ethnic and economic issues, but the issue of making Sinhala the national language proved so unpopular among Burghers and Tamils that Bandaranaike lost the 1965 election.

The UNP returned to power, promoting agricultural production, but unemployment rose. Bandaranaike won the 1970 election to lead a coalition government, the United Front. The next year, reforms gave the state control of the economy and a new constitution. Ceylon became the Republic of Sri Lanka in 1972. Unfortunately, the reforms alienated the Tamil minority, in particular the educated unemployed, who demanded the creation of an independent Tamil state, Eelam.

The "united front" was falling apart, and in the 1977 election, the UNP once again sailed into power, led by Junius Richard Jayewardene. In 1978 the constitution was amended again. The country was renamed the Democratic Socialist Republic of Sri Lanka, and a presidential system of government was introduced, with the president serving as both head of state and head of the government. Jayewardene reversed government policies, promoting

Sirimavo Bandaranaike earned fame as the world's first woman prime minister.

free enterprise and liberalizing the economy. Foreign investment was promoted, and the economy grew. The Jayewardene government was reelected in 1982.

In mid-1983, Tamil guerrillas demanding an independent state began a campaign of terrorist attacks. The Sinhalese retaliated, rioting against the Tamils. This marked the beginning of a long period of ethnic strife.

In 1988 Jayewardene retired, and Ranasinghe Premadasa became president. In 1993 Premadasa was assasinated. His successor, D.B. Wijetunga, called for elections the next year, when the Peoples Alliance (PA) came to power, with Chandrika Kumaratunga as prime minister. Kumaratunga soon became Sri Lanka's first woman president, following in the footsteps of her mother, Sirimavo, who was the world's first woman prime minister.

J.R. Jayewardene, Sri Lanka's first president.

After seven years in power, the PA lost ground. In the 2001 election, the main opponent, the UNP, won just five seats short of a majority in the parliament. Sri Lanka now looks to the joint-leadership of Kumaratunga and the UNP's Ranil Wickremesinghe.

GOVERNMENT

SRI LANKA HAS A 60-YEAR TRADITION of democracy. The former British colony inherited a Westminster-style parliamentary system, with its first general elections held in 1947.

After independence Sri Lanka opted to stay within the Commonwealth of Nations as a free and sovereign state. In 1974 it became a republic, still within the Commonwealth. In 1978 a French-style presidential system of government was adopted.

The president of the Democratic Socialist Republic of Sri Lanka is head of state, chief executive, and supreme commander of the armed forces. He or she is elected by the people for a term of six years. The president appoints the prime minister, members of the cabinet, and court judges. He or she has the power to dissolve the parliament and call for a national referendum.

The president heads the executive branch of the government; the parliament holds legislative power. The judicial branch consists of the supreme court and a court of appeals.

In 1994 the newly elected President Chandrika Kumaratunga said that her government would propose constitutional reforms to devolve power from the presidency to the office of the prime minister. In 2000 a constitutional reform was proposed to do away with the executive presidency and reestablish a Westminster style of government, in which the parliament reigns supreme. Efforts in this direction have stalled.

Above: **Chandrika Kuma-ratunga was elected Sri Lanka's president in 1994 and again in 1999.**

Opposite: **The House of Parliament in Colombo.**

Right: **The new parliament complex in Sri Jayewardenepura Kotte was declared open in 1982 by then President Jayewardene.**

Below: **Young LTTE rebels.**

PARLIAMENT AND PROVINCES

Sri Lanka's legislative body is a unicameral, or single-house, parliament consisting of 225 members who are elected at the constituency or district level for a period of six years.

The Ministry of Provincial Councils and Local Government oversees nine provincial councils, whose members are elected for six-year terms. The president appoints provincial governors from outside the councils; ministers are selected from the pool of elected councilors. The provincial councils work with a network of 68 district councils. Municipal councils in the cities and urban councils in the towns answer to their respective provincial councils.

In 1987 the government agreed to give greater authority to the provinces. The provincial councils exercise their influence in such areas as rural development, education, health, and social services.

PRESIDENT CHANDRIKA BANDARANAIKE KUMARATUNGA (1994–)

Never in Sri Lanka had a leader risen to power with so much mass appeal—not counting the father of the nation, D.S. Senanayake—and been so unsuccessful in steering the country to peace and prosperity than during the presidency of Chandrika Bandaranaike Kumaratunga.

Kumaratunga is the second daughter of the late S.W.R.D. Bandaranaike—a former prime minister himself—and Sirimavo Bandaranaike—the world's first woman prime minister. Kumaratunga has a son and a daughter, both studying in Britain. Her actor-turned-politician husband, Wijaya Kumaratunga, met the same fate as her father—he was assassinated. A LTTE suicide bomber nearly killed Kumaratunga as well after a public meeting close to election day in 2000; she was blinded in one eye.

Kumaratunga led the PA coalition to success in 1994, winning a record 62 percent of the vote. She won the presidential election again in 2000, beating the chief opposition candidate, UNP's Ranil Wickremasinghe, the current prime minister. However, the ongoing civil war, an economic downturn, and corruption within her government have hurt Kumaratunga's popularity.

In a bid to gain support, in 2001 Kumaratunga entered into a deal with the Janatha Vimukthi Peramuna (JVP) party, the Sinhalese rebel party blamed for the murder of her husband. The JVP's demands include delaying talks with the LTTE.

PRESIDENT RANASINGHE PREMADASA (1988–93)

During his five years as president of Sri Lanka, Ranasinghe Premadasa embarked on a far-reaching program of economic and industrial development. In order to integrate the economy with the international market, trade policies were liberalized. Export-oriented industries were promoted in order to bring more foreign exchange into the country. Foreign investors were encouraged to set up industries in tax-free zones. In 1992 a "decade of exports" was declared, and geographic limits on tax-free zones were removed when the whole country was declared a tax-free Export Processing Zone (EPZ). State enterprises were privatized, or "peoplized," and workers became stockholders in these companies. Almost 10,000 employees from 23 privatized companies received free stock. Great efforts were made to promote employment. In 1992 Premadasa encouraged a project to establish 200 garment factories in rural areas, each providing 500 jobs.

While many government subsidies for the poor and unemployed were withdrawn, Premadasa's Janasaviya, or People's Power, program ensured that the poorest of the poor were given money to support themselves and start income-generating businesses. His other projects included the Gam Udawa, or Village Awakening, which set up a massive trade fair in remote areas and developed these areas, and the Million Houses Project. Also, under Premadasa, government officials carried out their business in rural areas. Premadasa was assassinated by an LTTE suicide bomber on May 1, 1993, as he was going to the May Day rally. He was succeeded by D.B. Wijetunge, who had served as prime minister.

Parliament in session.

THE VOTE REIGNS SUPREME

Sri Lankans are very politically conscious, having had the vote for more than 60 years. There are more than 12 million eligible voters in Sri Lanka and an abundance of newspapers in the three main languages—Sinhala, Tamil, and English—that reach even remote villages. Radio and television also bring news to the people islandwide.

Sri Lankans take their duty to vote very seriously. When the fiercely nationalistic Sinhalese JVP party attempted a boycott of the 1989/90 presidential and parliamentary elections through a terror campaign, threatening to kill the first seven voters at each polling booth, Sri Lankans still went to the polls to cast their ballots, no doubt trembling with fear. Even the 2001 election—one of the country's most violent—saw a high turnout. Around 50 deaths were reported during the election campaign, and the army and police were deployed to keep the peace on polling day.

In 1982, at the end of the UNP's first six-year term, Sri Lankans were asked to vote in a referendum: for a continuation of the government in power or for a general election. The first option won the vote. A national referendum is held before a major constitutional change can be made.

POLITICAL PARTIES

Political parties in Sri Lanka range from the democratic to the radical. The major ones are:

United National Party (UNP) D.S. Senanayake, independent Sri Lanka's first prime minister, led the UNP from its formation in 1946. The party won a major victory in 2001, and its leader Ranil Wickremesinghe was sworn in as the country's newest prime minister.

Sri Lanka Freedom Party (SLFP) S.W.R.D. Bandaranaike formed this breakaway party when he crossed over from the UNP to the opposition in the early 1950s. In 1956 the SLFP won a landslide victory, and Bandaranaike became prime minister. He was assassinated in 1959 and succeeded by his widow, Sirimavo Bandaranaike, the world's first woman prime minister.

Lanka Sama Samaja Party (LSSP) Formed in 1935, the LSSP is one of the oldest political parties. It was in the forefront of the struggle for independence and joined a coalition government for a couple of years in the 1960s; it has lost much of its clout now.

Communist Party (CP) Formed in 1943, this leftist party is part of the PA coalition. Its chairman for more than 40 years, Pieter Keuneman, died in 1997, and its current leader is Raja Collure.

The **Democratic United National Front (DUNF)** was formed in 1992 by two former cabinet ministers.

The **All-Ceylon Tamil Congress (TC)** and **Tamil United Liberation Front (TULF)** are two Jaffna-based political parties formed in the 1940s.

The **Sri Lanka Muslim Congress** was formed to protect the interests of Muslims in the Eastern province.

Janata Vimukti Peramuna (JVP) This Sinhalese rebel party terrorized the country and brought near anarchy under the leadership of its founder, Rohana Wijeweera, in 1971 and again in 1988. In 1989 the army executed Wijeweera. The party went underground until 1994 when it resurfaced and entered mainstream politics. In the 2000 election 10 party members were elected to parliament.

Liberation Tigers of Tamil Eelam (LTTE) Known the world over as a terrorist party, the LTTE has been fighting the government's armed forces for the last 18 years in an attempt to set up a separate Tamil state, called Eelam, in the north. The government outlawed the party in 1998, after the bombing where 16 people were killed at a sacred 16th-century Buddhist shrine.

ECONOMY

SRI LANKA traditionally has an agriculture-based economy, producing rice, rubber, tea, coconut, and many other plantation crops. Over the past two decades, however, industrial growth has made the manufacturing sector an important contributor to the Sri Lankan economy. Tourism is also a vital source of foreign earnings. Other sources of revenue are wages sent home by migrant workers and earnings from the export of manufactured garments and precious and semiprecious stones.

DIVERSIFICATION AND GROWTH

In 1977 the Jayewardene government implemented a growth policy that encouraged private enterprise in different sectors of the economy and promoted the growth of industry. This broadened the range of exports to include manufactured petroleum products, garments, gems, nontraditional commodities such as leather and rubber goods, minerals, even cut flowers and ornamental fish.

Between 1978 and 1983, economists pointed to Sri Lanka as an economic model. Growing at a rate of more than 8 percent, the Sri Lankan economy outpaced even developed countries. But the boom period ended when ethnic clashes broke out in 1983 between the Sinhalese and Tamils. Growth fell to 2.7 percent by 1988, then rose in 1990 to 6.2 percent, showing signs of another boom. But a downward trend followed instead, starting at 4.3 percent in 1992 and sliding to less than 1 percent in 2001.

Opposite: **Tea shrubs are grown on terraced slopes.**

Above: **Different kinds of tea grown in Sri Lanka.**

INDUSTRY AND FOREIGN INVESTMENT

The Air Lanka cargo terminal at the Katuna-yake EPZ.

Sri Lanka's manufacturing sector has made great strides in the past two decades. The textile and garment industry has been a star performer, while food processing and chemicals have also risen in importance. The government is looking to foreign investors to develop local industries. Companies pay lower taxes or no tax and enjoy duty-free imports for investments in selected industries, such as electronics.

The government has made efforts to build the country's infrastructure to attract foreign investment. There are three EPZs with paved roads, a reliable power and water supply, security systems, telecommunications, post offices, shipping agents, banking and customs services, medical clinics, and recreational facilities.

The LTTE is a threat to foreign investment. In 2001 Tamil Tigers attacked the air force base and international airport at Katunayake, destroying 10 aircraft and killing four air force personnel. Some foreign investors reacted by pulling out, and many factory workers lost their jobs.

A view of an EPZ from the air.

Gem-cutting is an industry the government promotes.

AGRICULTURE

The Mahaweli Dam aims to harness the power of Sri Lanka's longest river to generate electricity and to divert water from the river to the northern dry zone for agriculture.

Sri Lanka is primarily an agricultural society. More than 80 percent of the population work on small farms. Commercial crops accounted for over 90 percent of exports in 1970, but the figure had fallen below 20 percent by 1997. Sri Lanka's agricultural exports include tea, rubber, coconut, cocoa, coffee, tobacco, and spices such as pepper, cinnamon, cardamom, cloves, and nutmeg. Rice, fruit, and vegetables are grown for local consumption.

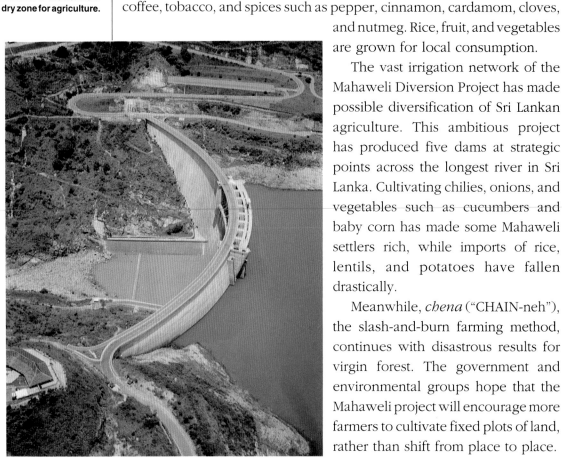

The vast irrigation network of the Mahaweli Diversion Project has made possible diversification of Sri Lankan agriculture. This ambitious project has produced five dams at strategic points across the longest river in Sri Lanka. Cultivating chilies, onions, and vegetables such as cucumbers and baby corn has made some Mahaweli settlers rich, while imports of rice, lentils, and potatoes have fallen drastically.

Meanwhile, *chena* ("CHAIN-neh"), the slash-and-burn farming method, continues with disastrous results for virgin forest. The government and environmental groups hope that the Mahaweli project will encourage more farmers to cultivate fixed plots of land, rather than shift from place to place.

A picker on a tea plantation. Tea leaves are processed on the estate. They are first withered by drying, then rolled to wring out the sap, fermented at a specific temperature, fired to dry, and finally graded. Processed tea leaves are packed in foil-lined chests and sold at tea auctions.

THE TEXTURE OF COCO-NUTTERY*

It is almost impossible for a visitor to leave Sri Lanka without seeing a coconut palm. Sri Lankans owe much of their lifestyle to the leaves, fruit, and even flowers of the coconut palm, which they call the "tree of life."

The **flowers** are used for decorative purposes at ceremonies. An oil lamp is placed in the inflorescence in a clay pot.

The **leaves** are often used in floral decorations. The creamy and supple young leaves can be trimmed, rolled, and folded into pretty shapes. The leaves of the coconut palm do have more essential uses, however, such as providing thatching for roofs. A bunch of mature leaf stalks, with their blades shaved off, makes an excellent broom when secured at the thicker end with a cord. The thicker part of the stalk, shaved clean and smooth and sharpened at one end, makes an excellent barbecue skewer. The leaves can also be braided into fans and screening mats.

The **nuts** are by far the most important part of the coconut palm, being both food and a cash crop. The coir—the thick, rough, fibrous outside layer—is woven into floor mats, tiles, or rope. The hard brown shell underneath the coir, when halved, may be used as a bowl for food or a large spoon or a container for collecting latex from rubber trees (another cash crop). The thick white kernel inside the shell is delicious: soft and slippery when young, hard and crunchy when mature. The latter is grated and squeezed for milk, which is added to curries, rice, and pancakes or made into desserts. Grated rather than dehydrated coconut forms the rich base of candy and other rich Sri Lankan sweets. The dried kernel, called copra, yields oil when pressed. Finally, in the hollow shell is the coconut water, a clear, sweet, thirst-quenching drink.

The **sap** of the coconut palm is used to make *thelijja* (TEL-lee-jah), a nonalcoholic drink, or toddy. A tapper (*above*) extracts the sap, which is then fermented for a few hours.

* Borrowed from Edward Lear, writer and artist

FISH, FLESH, AND FOWL

The fishing season is controlled by the monsoons. Fishermen stay on the southwestern beaches during the northeast monsoon and move to the northeastern coast during the southwest monsoon. Several inland fisheries have been set up with Japanese aid.

Ethnic clashes in the north and east have led to soaring prices for fish. As a result, many poor families have been deprived of a major source of protein. Cattle are more often reared for their milk and to do farm work than for their meat. They draw carts, plow fields, and help farmers thresh harvested rice stalks. Beef is eaten, but as Buddhists believe that life is precious and Hindus hold the cow sacred, the slaughter of cattle is decreasing.

Chicken runs (enclosures where chickens are raised for profit) are becoming popular; even housewives are starting them to supplement the family income.

Above: **Catamarans are used for fishing. The outriggers help balance the craft.**

Left: **The stilt fishermen of Welligama sit for hours on a narrow perch and may catch only a dozen fish a day.**

47

TOURISM

Tourism is an important foreign exchange earner for Sri Lanka. From 192,000 in 1978, tourist arrivals to the island reached 407,000 in 1982. However, ethnic conflict since 1983 has made it dangerous for foreigners to visit the country. After the island welcomed 400,414 visitors in 2000, the LTTE dealt another blow to tourism by attacking the airport at Katunayake in 2001. Sri Lanka's big attractions are its beaches, ancient cities, wildlife, charming rural areas, and famous hospitality. Also, the government is promoting the country as a convention center, with the $3 million Bandaranaike Memorial International Conference Hall, reputedly one of the best conference complexes in South Asia.

The finest gemstones in the world are found in Sri Lanka.

GEMS

Among the natural treasures of Sri Lanka are precious and semiprecious gems, which have attracted traders from all over the world for centuries. Sri Lanka's gems are part of the reason the island has been called the "Jewel of the Indian Ocean." Historical records show that Sri Lankan gems have been mined and fashioned into fine jewelry for more than 2,500 years. Sri Lanka has deposits of as many as 50 of the 140 varieties of gemstones in the world. Among the best-known are blue sapphires, rubies, topaz, zircons, garnets, amethysts, moonstones, quartz, and tourmaline. Today, Sri Lanka has one of the fastest-growing gem-cutting and gem-finishing industries in the world. More than 30,000 skilled gem cutters are employed nationwide. The government has provided tax incentives for entrepreneurs and has established a training center for gem cutting to increase the pool of skilled workers to promote the industry.

LOOKING FOR WORK

The unskilled in Sri Lanka have few options when it comes to earning a living. Some live just outside Colombo in shanty towns and do casual labor, such as loading and cleaning, in the commercial district. Those in the rural areas sell fruit and other food items on the streets (*above*). Many unemployed Sri Lankans register at agencies to find work as housemaids, babysitters, drivers, and the like in the Middle East and other Asian countries. These individuals have to be healthy and physically fit in order to work the long hours required, often 15 to 16 hours a day. The usual contract is for two years, and this may be renewed once, several times, or after an interval, depending on the work permit rules of the foreign country.

The government encourages the unemployed to seek work opportunities abroad. There are about a million Sri Lankans working abroad. Those with skills go to the Middle East, Australia, the United States, and western Europe. The Bureau of Foreign Employment, set up 10 years ago, trains domestic workers who migrate to West Asian countries and introduces them to conditions they will meet in their host countries. The bureau, with several non-governmental organizations and trade unions, now helps returned migrants start income-generating projects at home, to avoid the social consequences of broken homes and school dropouts. Migration of women workers is discouraged for the same reason.

EDUCATION AND EMPLOYMENT

Before colonization, Buddhist monks were the only teachers on the island. During the colonial period, schools run by Portuguese Roman Catholic and Dutch and British Protestant missions were favored by those aspiring to jobs in the government service.

In the 1960s Sinhala was made the national language. This, it is thought, was the major cause of ethnic strife instigated by the Tamil minority. English is now being given recognition and emphasis.

Education is free. The literacy rate is 92 percent for men and 90 percent for women, the highest by far in South Asia. More girls attend schools and universities than do boys. Women may enter any profession, even the air force, and they have risen to the top of their professions in the public sector. The private sector, however, still seems to prefer male chief executive officers. In the lower pay scales of the labor market, women have the more menial jobs, like plucking tea leaves on estates and running machines in garment factories.

JANASAVIYA—PEOPLE'S POWER

Sri Lanka is a socialist and near-welfare state, with government policies that financially support the poor. For example, the Janasaviya program was started in 1989 to provide poor families with a monthly subsidy for food and other essentials.

With the defeat of the UNP in 1994, the Janasaviya program—the party's brainchild—was renamed Samurdhi (prosperity) by the PA. Samurdhi gives a five-member family earning less than about US$8 a month a subsidy of around US$5. However, Sri Lanka aims to reduce the number of welfare recipients in the country, keeping only the poorest of the poor covered by the program.

HEALTH SERVICES

Sri Lanka has a free health service, with a network of hospitals and
dispensaries spread over the island. There are also private hospitals and
clinics for those who can afford the charges.

ENVIRONMENT

SRI LANKA HAS A HIGH LEVEL of biological diversity due to variations in topography and climate in the country. In addition, many of the island's plants and animals are indigenous. Some 23 percent of flowering plants and 16 percent of mammals in Sri Lanka are unique to this island, a biodiversity "hotspot."

In ancient times, Sri Lanka's natural environment was protected by royal decree. Following the teachings of the Buddha, all life was declared sacred, and animals lived in sanctuaries. One of the five daily precepts Buddhists continue to observe today is to avoid harming living things, including plants.

Large-scale destruction of Sri Lanka's flora and fauna began during colonial times. Forests were felled to make way for plantations, and animals were shot for sport or trade.

Post-independence development decimated forests to accommodate village expansion and urban sprawl. Elephants in particular suffered the loss of their natural habitat, as jungle was converted to sugarcane plantations. Herds were displaced and, as a result, they began rampaging through cultivated land. Farmers reacted in turn by killing these noble animals in an attempt to protect their crops.

The Sri Lankan government is leading conservation efforts, and laws are in place to protect the island's wildlife. The Ministry of Forestry and Environment (MFE) is in charge of environmental affairs on the national level. Operating under the MFE's wing are the Central Environmental Authority (CEA), which carries out environmental impact studies and controls air, water, and soil pollution, and the Department of Forestry, which looks after the management and conservation of natural forest.

Above: **Orchids grow in the dense southwestern tropical rain forests.**

Opposite: **Coconut trees swaying in the breeze are a common sight in Sri Lanka.**

More than
half of the tree
and mammal
population in the
Sinharajah is
endemic. The
reserve protects
several rare
reptiles, such as
the rough-nose
horned lizard.
Indigenous fish
such as the stone
sucker and tiger
loach swim in
the streams
that drain the
Sinharajah soil.

FORESTS

At the start of the 20th century, 75 percent of Sri Lanka was covered by dense forest. Large areas were cleared during the colonial years to make way for coffee, tea, and rubber plantations. Deforestation has continued to the present day, and less than 20 percent of the island remains under forest cover, mainly in the reserves.

The kind of vegetation that grows in a particular place depends on the area's topography, climate, and soil. Sri Lanka, with its hills and plains, monsoon seasons, and dry and wet zones, exhibits a diversity of forest types—tropical rain forests and dry-zone forests, mangrove swamps and coastal vegetation, mountain forests, scrublands, and grasslands.

The most common forest type on the island is semi-evergreen forest, largely in the dry zone. Though these forests consist mainly of evergreen trees, they also have some deciduous trees. In the wet zone, vegetation type varies by altitude. Wet evergreen forests, or rain forests, grow both in the lowlands and in the hills. Grasslands cover a small part of the lowlands. Mangroves and marshes grow in bays on the coast, while swamps flourish in freshwater areas.

Apart from illicit felling and selective logging, development projects, such as colonization programs to resettle people from the congested towns to cleared jungle areas, harm the forests' chances of survival. The building of dams affects river vegetation, while aquaculture destroys mangrove swamps. Shifting, or *chena*, cultivation is one cause of the disappearance of natural vegetation in the dry areas. A *chena* cultivator clears a piece of virgin forest by burning. When the ash has settled, the farmer grows vegetables and fruit and sows grain that needs little water. He works the area for two years before moving on to a fresh patch of land to begin the cycle again.

THE LION AND THE ELEPHANT

The Sinharajah forest reserve occupies an area of 34 square miles (89 square km) in the Sabaragamuwa and Southern provinces. Most of the forest was declared a reserve in 1875. In 1937 John Baker described the Sinharajah as "the only considerable patch of virgin tropical rain forest in the island." It remains Sri Lanka's last large tropical lowland rain forest.

The history of the forest is tied in legend to the history of the Sinhalese, descendants of a mighty lion and a princess. The word *sinharajah* ("SING-hah-RAH-jah") means "lion king." The name may also refer to the large size of the forest or to its previous royal status as land belonging to the ancient kings. Yet another legend tells that the forest was the last refuge of the lion, which no longer exists on the island.

In 1971 the government began a selective logging project to extract timber from the forest for the sawmill at Kosgama, 53 miles (85 km) northwest. Largely due to public pressure, in 1977 logging was banned in the forest. The next year the forest was declared a biosphere reserve, and in 1989, it made the UNESCO list of Natural World Heritage Sites.

The elephant orphanage at Pinnewela, a 30-minute drive from Kandy, is home to more than 60 elephants of different ages. The orphanage was set up to care for baby elephants whose mothers had been killed or trapped in the wild. Injured and displaced elephants can also find refuge at the orphanage, and calves have been bred in captivity. Visitors to Pinnewala get to see elephant herds taking a bath in the river (*below*) or baby elephants guzzling milk from gigantic feeding bottles.

FAUNA

Sri Lanka is home to 86 mammal species, including the elephant, jackal, bear, wild boar, buffalo, sambar, and the langur monkey.

The leopard is the island's top predator. No lions or tigers steal its kill, as happens to leopards in Africa and India. The Sri Lankan leopard knows no bounds. It ranges from the Horton Plains to the wet zone forests and sometimes ventures near upcountry estates.

Over 400 species of birds have been sighted in Sri Lanka; 26 are indigenous species. Most are resident, like the spot-billed pelican, but some migrate seasonally. More than 450 fish species, including the black ruby and cherry barb, red-tailed goby, and green pufferfish, populate Sri Lanka's rivers, marshes, and coastal waters.

There are more than 100 reptile species, 75 endemic. Sri Lanka's reptiles include the star tortoise, marsh crocodile, and five species of turtle, all protected. Snakes abound in the forests, the lethal species being the cobra, Russell's and saw-scaled viper, and Indian and Ceylon krait.

Sri Lanka is an amphibian hotspot, with more than 250 species of frogs—about 10 percent of all frog species in the world.

CONSERVATION

Providing refuge to so many species of indigenous wildlife, some of which are facing extinction, Sri Lanka's ecosystems need to be protected. The Department of Wildlife Conservation and the Department of Forestry look after the country's national parks and other protected areas, the latter focusing on forest reserves.

The Coast Conservation Department works to reduce coastal damage. Erosion is a particularly serious problem on the southern beaches, which face the Indian Ocean and are hit by waves from the open sea. Coral reefs serve as natural breakwaters, but scuba diving, coral mining, and other human activities pollute and damage the reefs.

Environmental groups have been set up in more than 3,000 schools across the island to nurture an environmentally friendly generation of Sri Lankans. By taking part in projects and writing reports, children learn about managing and protecting the environment and about living in an environmentally responsible way.

Above: **Waves break on a beach in Sri Lanka.**

Opposite: **The sambar is a species of deer that roams the Horton Plains. Standing just about 3 feet (1 m) tall, it has dark brown fur and distinctive three-point antlers.**

Rising sea levels will have a significant impact on the coast, where many of Sri Lanka's large cities are located. The population in the belt extending from Waikkal to Galle is projected at 8.4 million in 2010. Over 70 percent of the island's tourism infra-structure, two major ports (Colombo and Galle), and five fishery harbors are also located in this region. It is projected that sea levels will rise by about 11.8 inches (30 cm) by 2010.

POLLUTION AND FLOODING

The main environmental problems Sri Lanka faces include urban air pollution and water pollution, erosion and flooding, and indiscriminate garbage disposal.

Factories are required by law to obtain a license from the CEA before starting operations. The CEA grants a license after checking that proper pollution control systems are in place. Existing plants without such systems are expected to install them within a specified period. There is a growing market for pollution prevention equipment.

Deforestation, the disappearance of forest cover, leads to river bank erosion, increasing the severity of floods that are already a problem because of shifting coastal sand bars and lagoons that affect river exits to the sea. Deforestation and climate change are expected to gradually increase the frequency of drought, especially in the dry zone.

Many parts of the country lack the infrastructure and resources for waste management. The large towns depend on municipal garbage collectors, while in Colombo, a private firm sees to the cleanliness of the city. Uncontrolled dumping is a widespread occurrence, creating breeding grounds for pests such as rats and mosquitoes. Open dumping in nature areas pollutes ground and surface water, while open burning of waste contributes to air pollution, posing serious health threats.

A public health inspector assigned by the Ministry of Health sees to solid waste management in the municipal and urban councils. At the national level, the MFE and CEA draw up and enact policies concerning solid waste. The National Environmental Act restricts waste emission, while the local authorities are responsible for the proper removal of municipal solid waste and its disposal at suitable dumping areas.

Opposite: **Hydroelectric power is a major source of energy in Sri Lanka.**

ENERGY

Lacking fossil fuel reserves, Sri Lanka relies heavily on hydroelectric power. At least 70 percent of the country's electricity is derived from water power, while the rest comes from thermal power generated using imported oil.

While hydroelectric power is a clean form of energy, it has its shortcomings. It relies on the volume and strength of rivers, and power cuts have to be imposed whenever the southwest monsoon fails.

Sri Lanka intends to survey its territorial waters for oil deposits. Surveys in the early 1980s indicated possible offshore oil and gas reserves, but economic and political troubles prevented further exploration at the time. Sri Lanka is also looking to solar energy, and there is a wind power plant at Hambantota.

Sri Lanka has declared 1999 to 2009 as the decade of power development. New power plants and a modern national grid need to be built in order to provide every household with access to electricity and increase the efficiency of power distribution. The government is attracting private investors to the power sector, controlled by the Ceylon Electricity Board, by providing tax breaks and other incentives.

SRI LANKANS

SEVERAL ETHNIC GROUPS make up the Sri Lankan population of over 19 million. The main groups are the Sinhalese, Tamils, Moors, Burghers, and Veddhas. Other smaller groups make up the minority.

Sri Lankans from each ethnic group can be identified by their names. The most common names among the Sinhalese are Perera and Fernando. Other Sinhalese names such as Senanayake and Bandaranaike are as polysyllabic as Tamil ones such as Selvarajah and Kandasamy.

The Moors typically name their sons Mohammed and Ahmed and their daughters Fathima and Noor. The Burghers have Portuguese- or Dutch-sounding names such as Jansz and Buultjens.

The Sinhalese have an Indo-Aryan ancestry, the Tamils a Dravidian ancestry, the Moors an Arab ancestry, and the Burghers a European ancestry. By faith, the Sinhalese, Tamils, Moors, and Burghers are generally Buddhist, Hindu, Muslim, and Christian respectively.

More than 70 percent of Sri Lankans live in rural areas, since much of the country is given to agriculture. Most Sinhalese live in the southwest; Sri Lankan Tamils in the north and east; and Indian Tamils in the south-central region.

Almost 30 percent of Sri Lankans live in urban clusters—Colombo in the west, Kandy in the south-central hills, Galle in the south, and Jaffna in the north. The number of migrants to cities and industrial zones is rising.

With a falling birth rate and low death rate, the proportion of young dependents (below age 15) in the population is falling while that of old dependents (above age 64) is rising. Aging is thus a growing concern in the 21st century.

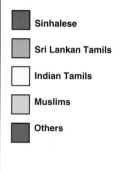

■ Sinhalese

■ Sri Lankan Tamils

□ Indian Tamils

■ Muslims

■ Others

Opposite: **Children near Sigiriya.**

Above: **Sri Lanka's ethnic groups.**

**Sri Lankan Tamils in
Jaffna.**

ETHNIC UNREST

Racism has plagued Sri Lanka for the past two decades. In fact, ethnic rivalry existed even before independence, under the divide-and-rule policy of the British. More English schools were set up in the north, especially in Jaffna. As a result, more Tamils benefitted from an English education, which put them in a better position to be admitted to universities and to study science, medicine, and mathematics. When the British left in 1948, Tamils held most of the well-paid positions in professions such as medicine, engineering, and accounting. (In the 1960s the government tried to close the ethnic gap with a quota system for university entrance. This naturally upset the Tamils.)

In 1956 the Bandaranaike government made Sinhala the official language of the country. Then in 1958, in response to objections from the Tamils, the government enacted the Reasonable Use of Tamil Act. Tamil became the language used by the administration in the north, in addition to Sinhala used nationally. Tamil and Sinhalese students have received instruction in their respective mother tongues in most schools and universities since 1961.

The emergence of the LTTE fueled ethnic unrest. In 1983 the LTTE killed 13 Sinhalese soldiers. Outraged, the Sinhalese community killed hundreds of Tamils and destroyed Tamil homes and shops. The Tamils turned to the LTTE to fight back, and hatred flared between the ethnic groups. Civil war broke out, and the fighting has gone on ever since.

The government has attempted to negotiate a settlement, granting the Tamils several concessions, short of an independent state called Eelam. The LTTE has assassinated several Sinhalese leaders and has made an attempt on the life of President Kumaratunga.

Happily, day-to-day encounters between Tamils and Sinhalese are friendly. They study and work together. Even on the outskirts of the area held by the LTTE, Sinhalese and Tamils help one another harvest the rice fields. In a bid to reduce ethnic division, English is being given prominence, even as a medium of instruction in schools. News is published and broadcast in Sinhala, Tamil, and English. Yet the LTTE and, in turn, the armed forces and politicians, keep the flames of war burning.

Trellis house on a "Moor" street. Every Sri Lankan city has a district or street with a Muslim character.

THE SINHALESE

The Sinhalese are descended from the ancient Indo-Aryans of northern India. The legend of Vijaya traces the origin of the Sinhalese to the prince whose father was Sinhabahu. The word *sinha* means "lion," and the Sinhalese like to think they have a leonine ancestry.

The Sinhalese inherited the Indian caste system. One's caste determined one's profession as goldsmith, dancer, tom-tom beater, farmer, fisherman, or clothes washer, called *dhoby* ("DHOH-bee"). Farmers belonged to a high caste, just below the aristocracy. But Buddhism broke caste barriers, and the Sinhalese now generally ignore caste in work, though not in marriage.

Most urban Sinhalese wear Western-style clothing to work. At home and in the streets and shops, the men wear a shirt over a *sarama* ("SAH-rah-mah"), a piece of cloth wrapped around the lower body from the waist almost to the ankles. The traditional dress for women is the *sari* ("SAH-ree"). Rural Sinhalese women wear a blouse and a printed wrap-around. Gold jewelry is a must.

THE TAMILS

Sri Lankan Tamils, commonly known as "Jaffna Tamils," live mostly in the north and east of the country, although major towns in other areas also have large Tamil populations. Sri Lankan Tamils claim descent from the Chola, Pandya, and Pallava invaders from southern India. They are Hindus and adhere to the caste system more rigidly than do the Sinhalese.

Sri Lankan Tamils see themselves as superior to Indian Tamils, who are descendants of the workers imported from India by the British to work on tea and coffee plantations during the colonial years. Indian Tamils live mostly on the tea estates in the south-central hills.

At home, Tamil men may wear a *verti* ("VER-tee"), similar to a *sarama*, with a collarless shirt. Tamil women, like Sinhalese women, wear the *sari*. Married women wear a *thali* ("TAH-lee"), a pendant symbolizing the marriage vow, and a *pottu* ("PAW-too"), a red dot on the forehead that is associated with fertility. The hair parting is also colored red. Most Tamil women wear jasmine flowers in their hair at weddings and other functions.

Opposite: **A Sinhalese girl.**

Below: **A Jaffna Tamil in prayer.**

Above: **Two Burgher girls.**

Opposite: **A Muslim man in his shop.**

MOORS AND BURGHERS

Moors, descendants of Arab traders who settled in Sri Lanka as long ago as the eighth century A.D., live in all parts of the island except in Jaffna. Apart from Moors, descendants of migrant Malays from Southeast Asia make another Muslim group in Sri Lanka.

Burghers divide themselves into groups according to their ancestry— there are Dutch Burghers, British Burghers, and Portuguese Burghers. They live in urban areas (the Dutch word *burgher* means "town dweller") and follow a Western lifestyle.

When Sinhalese nationalism swept through the land in the 1950s, and Sinhala and then Tamil, rather than English, were adopted as the languages of instruction in schools, many Burgher families emigrated, mainly to Australia.

VEDDHAS

The aboriginal Veddhas live in the forests of the Uva basin east of the
south-central hills. They have short curly hair and broad noses, like the
aboriginal bushmen of Australia and pygmies of Africa.

The Veddhas call themselves Wanniya-laeto, or "forest dwellers." The
name *veddha* ("VAYD-hah") is Sinhala for "hunter." Once believers in
spirits, many Veddhas have now converted to Buddhism. They are fast

losing their identity as hunter-gatherers, as they are resettled in villages and forced to give up hunting. Instead, they cultivate land on the jungle fringes, living on game, honey, and the produce of their plots.

In the late 1970s, the government began clearing Veddha ancestral lands to make way for the Mahaweli Diversion Project. In 1983 more land was taken from the Veddhas and turned into the Maduru Oya National Park.

Due to international interest in the plight of the Veddhas, the government declared in 1998 that the Veddhas could return to their ancestral land.

However, returning Veddhas have found intruders, such as poachers and loggers who rob the forest of game and timber.

GYPSIES

The gypsies live in groups of a few families under a leader. They are nomadic, living in temporary shelters made out of leaves and loading their clothes, cooking pots, chickens, and other belongings on the backs of donkeys when traveling to a new location.

A Veddha boy with a hunting rifle.

The gypsies have their own system of government, with a chief justice in Anuradhapura. They meet annually to discuss matters such as travel routes. Each group specializes in a craft or service. For example, the Ahikuntakaya trap snakes and charm them with the movement (not the music) of their pipes. Other groups may carve their niche in tattooing, telling fortunes, making beads, hats, or reed baskets, training monkeys to dance, and so on.

LIFESTYLE

THE ANCESTRAL HERITAGE of each of Sri Lanka's ethnic groups has given them different customs and practices that have been passed down from one generation to the next. The different faiths that the Sinhalese, Tamils, Moors, and Burghers profess have also greatly influenced their behavior. In addition, the villager and the urbanite adhere to tradition to varying degrees.

Since Sri Lankans have different lifestyles and patterns of behavior, it is nearly impossible when describing any one group of Sri Lankans to say, "*This* is the lifestyle of the Sri Lankan." However, there are certain values that the different ethnic groups share.

For example, all Sri Lankans take pride in their families. The Sri Lankan family unit is close-knit and often an extended family, in which a young couple lives under one roof with their parents, aunts, uncles, grandparents, and sometimes even great-grandparents.

Children are doted on. Babies are hardly ever left to cry; they are indulged as much as possible. Wealthy couples used to employ *ayahs* ("AH-yahs"), or "nannies," to take care of their children.

Today, however, young working mothers often put their careers on hold to look after their young children. They are entitled to 84 days paid maternity leave for the first two children and 42 days for the third and subsequent. In any case, the relatives are often around to lend a hand.

Other "Sri Lankan" values are respect, hospitality, impetuosity, and cleanliness.

Opposite: **A rare sight in present-day Sri Lanka—residents of Udappuwa, a coastal town in the dry zone, dig into a sandy beach to reach fresh water.**

Below: **Two generations apart.**

Opposite: **Baths are soothing in Sri Lanka's hot climate. The nearest facility may sometimes be an open stream.**

SHARED VALUES

RESPECT Another value Sri Lankans share is respect for the elderly. Families take good care of their old relatives and make efforts to ensure that they feel wanted. There are retirement homes for the elderly, of course, but it is usually people with no relatives who live in these homes. Those with a family are seldom left to live alone. Sri Lankan children are brought up with the idea that it is their duty to care for their parents. Buddhism, a major religion in Sri Lanka, emphasizes this duty.

Showing respect extends to other seniors and people of higher social status as well. Children respect their parents, students respect their teachers, and society respects monks, nuns, and priests. When talking to a monk, one shows respect by folding the hands in prayer and bowing. One does not touch a monk.

Students show their school principal respect by standing up when the principal walks into the classroom. On the first day of school, a student may greet the teacher with a sheaf of betel leaves and kneel, palms closed. The same salutation is made when greeting one's parents at the new year or when inviting relatives to one's wedding.

HOSPITALITY Sri Lankans can be hospitable or irritable, depending on the time and place. Waiting in a bus line or weaving through a shopping crowd, for example, people may find it hard to avoid an argument and may react "as if a fly went past the nose," to use the Sinhala saying. (Sri Lanka in the hot season is full of flies.)

People tend to calm down and feel more relaxed at home. No matter how humble, the home is invariably a place for sharing and caring. Visitors are always invited to stay for a meal, and foreign guests are treated with special graciousness.

IMPETUOSITY Sri Lankans can also be impetuous. Bets taken during parliamentary elections range from shaving one's head to giving away all one's possessions. A party can start anytime, anywhere. Traveling on a train, one is likely to suddenly hear the latest popular Hindi song blaring from a tape recorder and see young people dancing in the car.

CLEANLINESS Cleanliness is godliness to most Sri Lankans. Sri Lankans are avid bathers, probably because the weather is tropical and cool water is plentiful. Streams, rivers, beaches, and swimming pools are always crowded.

BIRTH THROUGH CHILDHOOD

Every pregnancy is regarded as a blessing in Sri Lanka. The island may be overpopulated, the government may encourage family planning, but to any family, a new baby is always welcome. A pregnant woman is likely to be fussed over by her family, who will try to allay her craving for an exotic or unusual food. Her mother, grandmother, or mother-in-law will supervise her meals. Her colleagues and friends will shower her with pickles, chutney, and fresh fruit.

The baby is usually delivered in a hospital or maternity home. Even villages have their own maternity homes. There was a time when births took place at home, with a midwife in attendance. Infant mortality was high then. It is not the custom in Sri Lanka to throw a baby shower, but visitors bring gifts for the baby soon after birth.

FIRST RICE AND FIRST LESSON Tamil and Sinhalese parents make a ritual of a baby's first meal of boiled rice. This usually happens when the baby is around eight months old. Hindus feed the baby the first mouthful of milk rice in the *kovil* ("KOH-vil"), or Hindu temple.

The Sinhalese lay a mat on the floor with dishes of *kiributh* ("ki-ri-booth")—milk rice, bananas, traditional sweets, a book, and a piece of jewelry. The baby is allowed to crawl on the mat and choose one item. If the baby reaches for the book, everyone says they are in the presence of a future scholar or intellectual. If the piece of jewelry is picked, the baby shows promise of wealth and prosperity. If an item of food is grabbed, everyone fears the baby will become a bum!

At about the age of 2, the child has his or her first lesson. The lesson is given at a predetermined auspicious hour by a learned relative, the temple monk, or the principal of the local school.

GROWING UP

Traditionally, a family celebration marked each milestone in the life of the individual. Sharing personal experiences with family members, especially parents, helped to strengthen bonds. But many families now ignore the rituals that form part of such celebrations.

A Sinhalese or Tamil girl celebrates her coming of age and eligibility for marriage with her family. In a traditional Tamil home, the young girl stays in seclusion for about 16 days. In a traditional Sinhalese home too, she avoids normal activity, and it is considered bad luck for her to look upon a male, even a brother. Then at the appointed time, the girl is bathed by a *dhoby*, who pours water over her from a clay pot and then dashes the pot to the ground. The girl receives gifts, often cash or jewelry.

There is no special ceremony for a boy attaining puberty, unless he is Muslim, in which case he is circumcised in his early teens.

Below: **A Sri Lankan Tamil girl.**

MARRIAGE PROPOSALS

The following are two separate print ads for a marriage partner.

BRIDE Respectable Govi Buddhist parents seek for their pretty BSc. qualified daughter, 27, a professionally qualified partner preferably an engineer, doctor, or person of similar status. Assets over 1.5 million. Send horoscope with details.

BRIDEGROOM Tamil-origin Hindu, now employed as a chief accountant in Qatar, aged 42, widower, seeks a simple and kind-hearted partner. Religion, caste, race immaterial. Widows and divorcees without encumbrances considered. All details in first letter.

MARRIAGE

Married life is the preference for most Sri Lankan women; staying single is not an option. While teen marriages used to be common, Sri Lankans now marry at a later age for economic reasons.

Arranged marriages are still a strong tradition in Sri Lanka. Originally, a marriage broker called the *magul kapuwa* ("MAH-gool KAH-poo-wah") would visit the parents of an eligible young man or woman and help the parents "fix up" their son or daughter. These days, with the *magul kapuwa* almost extinct, Sri Lankans turn to relatives and friends for assistance in matchmaking and to advertising in the newspapers for potential wives and husbands.

Marriage mediators propose candidates and investigate their morals and credentials. Dowries are settled discreetly. Though the groom would like his bride to bring a dowry, he prefers not to ask for it. It is up to the bride's parents to endow her with cash, jewelry, and a house. A Tamil custom even allows the man to use part of his wife's dowry to settle his own sister in marriage.

Wedding celebrations are a big affair. A village wedding may last for days, while the urban rich patronize big hotels. Most couples prefer to invite only their closest relatives and friends to their home. The tradition is for the couple to go to the groom's home after the celebration in the bride's home, and the bride's immediate family visits her the next day. There is also a post-honeymoon party at the groom's home.

Tamils usually marry in the temple, but if the wedding is in a hotel, a priest performs the ceremony before the guests. Muslims celebrate the wedding at the bride's home or at a hotel. Burghers marry in church and hold a reception after the ceremony. Many Christian Sinhalese follow the same practice.

Opposite: **The elaborate traditional dress of a Kandyan bridegroom.**

THE WEDDING CEREMONY

There is an auspicious time, chosen by an astrologer, for every step of a Sinhalese Buddhist wedding ceremony. The couple gets married in a *poruwa* ("POH-roo-wah"), a decorated structure like a house. The bride's maternal uncle guides the rituals. The little fingers of the groom's left and the bride's right hand are tied together with gold thread, and water from a silver urn is poured over the knot to symbolize sharing. The bride is dressed in rich silks and lots of jewelry. A Kandyan bride wears the traditional seven *padakkam* ("PAH-dah-kum"), or pendants, starting with a choker and ending with a chain reaching the knees. The items of jewelry she wears are heirlooms; her family may go into debt just to dress her on her wedding day.

HOROSCOPES: ANCIENT CONSULTANT

A horoscope is cast by an astrologer, who takes the time of birth as the basis for prediction. The time of birth determines the zodiac sign, as well as whether the person is *deva* ("DAY-veh"), *manussa* ("mah-NOOS-seh"), or *raksha* ("RUK-shah), meaning godly, human, or devilish, respectively.

Horoscopes are written on a chart or an *ola* ("OH-lah") scroll made of a cured piece of talipot palm leaf. Good and bad periods in a person's life are recorded.

When a marriage is proposed, the horoscopes of the couple are compared as the very first step. If more than half of 20 "conditions" are favorable, the union can go through with no disastrous results.

Horoscopes are read by an astrologer at various stages and events in a person's life: at birth; at puberty; for an examination or a new job; when choosing a spouse; for a new house; or for any other important decision that has to be made. Horoscopes are a guide from the heavens.

HOROSCOPES AND AYURVEDIC MEDICINE

A horoscope becomes important when someone is ill and needs to consult an Ayurvedic doctor.

Folk medicine, or the use of herbal and traditional cures, is a thriving practice in Sri Lanka. So important is this 2,500-year-old practice that there are five times as many doctors practicing Ayurvedic medicine than Western medicine. There is even a government ministry responsible for Ayurvedic medicine.

An Ayurvedic cure treats the whole patient, not just the ailment. Even the person's horoscope and temperament are relevant. Herbs, roots, and spices are taken as medicine. A tea of ginger and coriander, for example, may be prescribed for the common cold.

It is commonly believed by Sri Lankans that when Western drugs fail, it is time to resort to Ayurvedic cures. Many Sri Lankans believe that both Western and Ayurvedic medicines can be used simultaneously. This is why pharmacies stock both Western drugs and Ayurvedic herbs. The World Health Organization acknowledges that both branches of medicine can learn much from each other.

Opposite: **A Sinhalese bride in a Westernized** *sari.* **Dressing a bride for her wedding is the work of design salons.**

DEATH AND FUNERALS

Buddhists and Hindus cremate their dead; Christians and Muslims bury theirs. However, many Christians are now opting for cremation.

When wood was cheap, a pyre of special timber was built. Now, gas crematoriums are used in big cities. Funerals in Sri Lanka tend to be expensive. Except for Muslims, who hold the funeral within 24 hours of a person's death, most Sri Lankans have their dead embalmed and keep the body in the house or funeral parlor for relatives and friends to pay their last respects. In villages, the entire community turns out to pay their respects to the deceased and to comfort the bereaved.

For economic reasons, however, funerals are becoming simpler, with the exception of state funerals for political figures and religious persons of high rank. Many non-Muslims now hold a funeral within a day of a person's death. Also, some people choose to have their bodies donated after death to a medical faculty for research, thus saving their families the expense of even a coffin.

Buddhists observe last rites for the dead called the *pansakula* ("PUN-seh-cool-leh"). Monks are invited to the cemetery or to the home where the body lies. They chant a verse in Pali that says all things are transient, all things decay and pass away. A sermon is preached to comfort the mourners, who give 60 feet (18 m) of white cloth to the temple.

The nearest relatives pour water from a jug into a bowl so that it spills over, signifying the transference of merit to the dead. The greater the merit, the better the chance of rebirth in a good place as a human being. Two nephews of the dead person circle the pyre or crematorium three times before the cremation. The day after the cremation, the ashes of the body are collected in a clay urn and later buried.

Dané ("DAH-neh"), meaning alms, are given to the temple on the seventh day after death. Three months later and on every anniversary of the death, monks are invited to the home of the bereaved for alms-giving. This is believed to confer merit on the dead person and also on the living, who by this act of giving lessen their craving for material things.

A Christian funeral consists of a service held in church, followed by the burial at the cemetery. The coffin is lowered into a hole in the ground, and those present throw handfuls of soil on the coffin, signifying "ashes to ashes, dust to dust."

Muslims carry their dead to the cemetery in a covered wicker stretcher and bury their dead without a coffin.

The few Zoroastrians in Sri Lanka leave their unburied dead to be consumed by vultures in a section of the cemetery set apart for this.

Burial in a coffin is a Christian practice. Muslims do not use a coffin, while Buddhists and Hindus cremate their dead.

A lawyer sits at his cluttered desk.

EMPLOYMENT

Sri Lankans can legally enter the labor market once they reach the age of 18. However, there are children illegally employed in households and on plantations, and the government is seeking to improve policy measures and raise public awareness on this issue.

The retirement age is 55, but senior workers may, at the employer's discretion, choose to continue in their positions beyond age 55.

Most Sri Lankans are employed in agriculture, and their jobs revolve around the seasons. Many plantation workers live "on site," in barrack-like quarters, often one family to a room.

The work pattern is more regular in urban areas, especially in the industrial and service sectors. Much of the labor force works in the tourism industry—in hotels, for transportation companies and arts and crafts shops, and at tourist attractions.

Office workers work eight to 10 hours a day, with a one-hour break. Saturday is a half day—five hours. The overtime wage rate is one-and-a-half times the normal rate, and everyone gets 14 days of paid vacation.

Women are employed in all sectors, but they dominate the lower-paying jobs. Tea-picking, one of the lowest-paid jobs, is mostly done by women. About 80 percent of the factory workers in the trade zones are young single women who live in nearby boarding houses.

Unemployment is a problem, particularly in the shanty towns around the larger cities such as Colombo. Slum occupants try to find work wherever they can, such as helping at shops as packers and loaders. Many of the unemployed have migrated to the United States, Europe, Southeast Asia, and the Middle East in search of work. In rural areas, the Sarvodaya movement addresses unemployment by awakening in villagers a sense of their own power and ability. A Sarvodaya work camp mobilizes the community to improve its own living conditions.

A barbershop, starkly simple, but decorated with pictures, some of Hindu gods.

RELIGION

FOUR MAJOR WORLD RELIGIONS are firmly rooted in Sri Lanka, and it is common to see Buddhist, Hindu, Muslim, and Christian dignitaries sitting on the same platform at important functions.

One result of the country's mixed religious heritage is that the faiths have borrowed rituals and symbols from one another. For example, the Buddha is believed to be one of the 10 reincarnations of Vishnu, a Hindu deity. The *thali*, the symbolic marriage necklace of Tamil Hindus, is also used by Sri Lankan Muslims. As for Sinhalese and Tamils who profess to be Christian—their ancestors having been converted by the Portuguese, Dutch, or British—the Sinhalese are influenced by Buddhist ethics, while Tamil Christians are influenced by their Hindu heritage.

Opposite: **A golden statue of the Buddha sits in the serenity of a temple in Sri Lanka.**

Left: **Monks walk past a Hindu temple door, shading themselves from the midday sun.**

The chief trustee of the tooth relic carries a replica of it in the Esala Perahera, an annual procession.

BUDDHISM

The Sinhala Dynasty, so legend says, was founded by Prince Vijaya the day the Buddha died in India. To Sri Lankans, this means they have an inherited role as protector of Buddhism. But it was really much later, about 250 B.C., that Buddhism came to Sri Lanka through Mahinda, the son of Emperor Asoka. A few significant events followed that entrenched the religion in Sri Lanka.

Asoka's daughter, Sanghamitta, brought a sapling from the *bo* tree under which Prince Siddhartha was sitting when he attained enlightenment. The princess founded the Bhikkuni Order, an order of nuns, in Sri Lanka.

In the fourth century A.D., Princess Hemamala of India escaped to Sri Lanka with the Buddha's sacred left eyetooth concealed in her hair. Subsequently, kingship went to whomever possessed the tooth relic. It is now protected and revered in the Dalada Maligawa, or Temple of the Tooth, in Kandy. A replica is paraded in Kandy once a year at the Esala Perahera. Another historic event was the writing of the sacred Buddhist scriptures on *ola* leaves at the Aluvihare temple cave in Matale, north of Kandy.

At various periods in Sri Lanka's history, while South Indian invaders pillaged stupas and temples and enthusiastic colonizers converted the local population, Buddhism was hidden away in isolated temples, protected and preserved by devout monks. Yet, from the third century B.C. until today, Theravada Buddhism in its purest form, adhering strictly to the original Pali preachings of the Buddha, continues to be practiced on the island.

The Dalada Maligawa in Kandy is where the Buddha's sacred tooth is enshrined.

HOW BUDDHISM CAME TO SRI LANKA

Around 250 B.C., while in hot pursuit of a deer in the Mihintale hills, close to his capital, King Devanampiya Tissa heard his name called. He stopped dead in his tracks. Who dared address him so familiarly? He saw a yellow-robed monk who introduced himself as Mahinda, son of Emperor Asoka. He had come from India to teach Buddhism to the people.

Mahinda tested the king with a riddle about mango trees, one not easily understood.

"King, what is this tree called?"

"It is an *amba* ("AHM-ba") tree." *(Amba* means "mango.")

"Besides this *amba* tree, is there any other *amba* tree?"

"There are many other *amba* trees."

"Besides this *amba* tree and those other *amba* trees, are there any other trees on earth?"

"There are many trees, but they are not *amba* trees."

"Besides the other *amba* trees and the trees that are not *amba*, is there any other?"

"Gracious Lord, this *amba*!"

Thus the king showed himself capable of understanding the *Dhamma* ("DHAHM-mah"), the truth revealed by the Buddha. Mahinda preached a sermon, and the king and his people became Buddhists. He accepted a royal invitation to live on the island, but rejected a magnificent temple in favor of his cave in Mihintale. After climbing 100 steps, one can still see his rock bed, his bathing pool, and the rock-hewn vessel used for his breakfast gruel.

A teacher instructs his students.

BUDDHIST WAYS

Buddhism is a way of life. Upon attaining enlightenment on the full moon night of the month of May, the Buddha realized four noble truths: the existence of suffering, its cause, its eradication, and the Eightfold Path to *Nibbana* ("nib-HAH-nah").

To Buddhists, the Buddha is a teacher and guide, a human being who found a way to self-deliverance. Buddhist statues, temples, shrines, and the sacred *bo* tree are venerated with offerings of flowers, the burning of incense symbolizing purity, and the lighting of oil lamps, symbols of wisdom and enlightenment. They are reminders of the Buddha's teaching that all things are impermanent.

The four Buddhist holy days, or *poya* ("POH-yeh") days, correspond with the phases of the moon. On a full-moon *poya* day, besides listening to sermons preached by the monks at the temple, Buddhists observe eight precepts—three more than usual on other days. They call for abstinence and simple living. Some Buddhists observe 10 precepts, the extra two being not to deal with money and not to wear ornaments.

FIVE AND EIGHT PRECEPTS

Buddhists observe these five precepts daily:
- not to destroy life
- not to take what is not given, i.e. not to steal
- not to behave immorally
- not to tell an untruth or slander
- not to take intoxicating drinks and drugs

In addition, on special days, Buddhists do not:
- eat at odd times and particularly not after midday
- use perfume and cosmetics, listen to music, or dance
- use luxurious chairs and beds

WORDS IN BUDDHISM

Bhikku   ("BIK-hoo") Monk.

Dané   ("DAH-nay") Alms-giving.

Nibbana   ("nib-HAH-nah") Nirvana, or the end of the samsaric cycle, when no further births take place. This is subsequent to attaining Enlightenment, as did the Buddha.

Nikaya   ("nik-HAH-yah") Buddhist sect of monks. The caste system exists among monks in the form of different sects. Their beliefs are the same, but their rituals and the way they wear their robes differ a little. Monks of the *Siyam Nikaya*, established in the mid-18th century, carry umbrellas and wear their robes only over one shoulder. Monks of the *Amarapura Nikaya* (since 1803) carry umbrellas and cover both shoulders. Monks of the *Ramanya Nikaya* (since 1835) carry a palm leaf shade and cover both shoulders. As the years of origin suggest, the latter two sects have broken away from the first through disagreement with its rules.

Pin   ("PIN") Merit. "Merit making" is like earning credits. The more merit a Buddhist makes, the greater the likelihood of rebirth into a better life after death. The Buddhist lay person makes merit by giving alms, meditating, and observing all the precepts.

Sangha   ("SUNG-hah") The monastic order.

HINDUISM

Hindus worship one or many gods according to personal choice or particular needs. Brahmin priests act as spiritual guides to Hindu devotees, who make ritual prayers and offerings of food, flowers, and lighted brass lamps daily and on special occasions.

The *Vedas*, a collection of more than a thousand hymns, are the Hindus' source of religious knowledge. Hindus believe in the caste system, which is strongly linked to reincarnation. They are content with their station in life, believing it to be the result of *karma* ("KAHR-meh"), the reward or punishment for good or bad deeds carried out in their previous lives. They try and do good deeds in this life so that their next life will be that of a high-caste person.

Sri Lankan Hindus worship the full pantheon of Hindu gods, including Brahma the creator; Shiva the destroyer of evil and ignorance; Parvati, wife of Shiva; their two sons, Skanda (or Murugan), the Kataragama god, and Ganesh; Pattini, goddess of health and chastity; and Vishnu, preserver of life. Aiyanar, who guards the forests, crops, tanks, and trees, is a most important god for Tamil farmers in the dry zone.

Most Sri Lankan Hindus are Shaivites —Shiva worshipers who believe in the impermanence of things. There is also a

At a wayside shrine, a Hindu sits in front of a screen that depicts Murugan and his two consorts.

good number of Vaishnavites—Hindus who believe in the supremacy of Vishnu—on the island.

Jaffna is the stronghold of Hinduism in Sri Lanka. Hindus worship at temples called *devale* ("DAY-veh-leh") and shrines called *kovil* ("KHOH-vil"). Hindu temples are designed like the human body, with a head, body, and feet. The temple's main statue is situated in the head, while offerings are made in the body, or stomach, of the temple. The *gopuram* ("goh-POO-rehm"), a multi-tiered gateway with carved images, is at the feet, where worshipers enter the temple.

A Hindu swami with streaks of prayer ash on his forehead. The way ash is placed indicates which god he worships.

ISLAM

Muslims are the most conservative religious group in Sri Lanka. They follow their customs strictly. Like Muslims everywhere, they fast during the month of Ramadan and aim to make a pilgrimage to Mecca at least once in their lives.

Muslims make no material offerings and have no images in their mosques. The words of the Koran guide their spiritual and moral lives, and the hypnotic voice of the *muezzin* ("moo-EZ-zin") calling the faithful to prayer five times a day keeps them constantly conscious of their faith.

Every city in Sri Lanka has its own Muslim section, so that Sri Lankan Muslims are never too far from a mosque; its location is marked from afar by a very visible minaret.

CHRISTIANITY

Christianity came to Sri Lanka with the European colonists, whose active conversion efforts established several denominations on the island, including Anglican, Methodist, Baptist, and Presbyterian.

Roman Catholicism is represented in the coastal areas. The vast majority of Burghers are Christian, and there are Sinhalese and Tamils who consider themselves Christians as well.

THE FOREST SHRINES OF KATARAGAMA

Buddhism does not encourage faith in gods and supplication to them. Yet many Buddhists in Sri Lanka go to Kataragama in the southeast of the island to invoke blessings on themselves. Hindus go there every year to make peace with the Hindu god of war, Skanda or Murugan, for this major god of Kataragama is believed to be fierce and vengeful.

Kataragama is a special place for many historical reasons. First, it is where King Devanampiya Tissa planted the sapling of the *bo* tree brought to Sri Lanka by Emperor Asoka's daughter. Next, King Aggabodhi, chief of Ruhuna, built a Buddhist temple and monastery at Kataragama in A.D. 661. Kataragama has also been the capital of several kings—Lokeswara, Kesadatu, and Vijaya Bahu I.

Several temples exist at Kataragama, including those dedicated to Valli Amma, Thevani Amma, Ganesh, and various other Hindu deities. Muslims from the surrounding villages flock to Kataragama to drink from a spring believed to be the fountain of life—its water is said to make those who drink it immortal. The waters of the Menik Ganga, a river that runs through the forest at Kataragama, are also believed to be sacred.

Sri Lankans have woven many legends around Kataragama. One tells of the Hindu war god, Skanda or Murugan, arriving in Sri Lanka and looking for a place to stay. He went first to the Tamils, who turned him away. He then went to the Sinhalese, who built him a shelter of leaves.

To punish the Tamils, Skanda decreed that they should come to Kataragama every year and torture themselves in fulfilling their vows. Thus it has been since that time, 2,000 years ago. Every year, Hindus undergo rituals of self-mortification, such as walking on hot coals or carrying on the shoulders a *kavadi* ("KAH-veh-di"), a wooden or metal arch decorated with peacock feathers.

Another legend tells of a prince who fell in love with Valli Amma, the daughter of a Veddha chief. Valli Amma rejected the prince, so his brother, knowing that Valli Amma feared elephants, planned to turn himself into one to frighten her so that the prince could come to her rescue and win her heart.

Disguised as a hermit and carrying a pot of magic water that he was to pour over his brother once the plan was carried out, the prince went to meet Valli Amma at Kataragama. But seeing that she was choking on her meal, he rushed to give her a sip of the magic water and dropped the pot. Then his brother appeared as an elephant, and the terrified Valli Amma agreed to go with the prince. Unfortunately, the magic water had been spilled, and the prince's brother could never regain his human form.

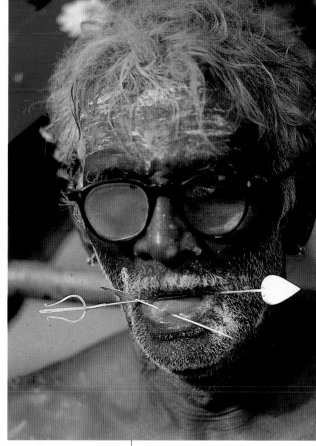

Body piercing is another Hindu sacrificial ritual.

සීගිරිය තානායම

சிகிரியா வாடிவீடு

SIGIRIYA
REST HOUSE

LANGUAGE

LANGUAGE IS A CONTROVERSIAL ISSUE in Sri Lanka. It has, from time to time, been manipulated for political ends. Even today, language is a point of division between Sinhalese and Tamils.

During the British colonial period English was the official language. This split Sri Lankans into the English-educated and those who spoke indigenous languages. In 1956 Sinhala became the official language. After much Tamil agitation, the 1978 constitution stated that Tamil would be a national language, though Sinhala would remain the official language.

Sinhala is the language of administration throughout Sri Lanka, but Tamil serves the same function in the northern and eastern parts of the country, where large Tamil populations reside. Schools have introduced a "link language," English, as a second language for all students, while Sinhala and Tamil are third languages for Tamil and Sinhalese children respectively. Most signboards and notices in Sri Lanka are in three languages: Sinhala, Tamil, and English.

Opposite: **A signboard in Sri Lanka's three main languages.**

Left: **Children walk to school in rural Sri Lanka.**

Centuries-old Sinhala script carved in stone in Matara.

SINHALA

Sinhala is spoken by 80 percent of the Sri Lankan population. Everyone in the country, except perhaps Western-educated urbanites, can communicate in Sinhala.

Old Sinhala had its origin in Prakrit, an ancient Indian language. In the second century B.C., the influence of Sanskrit changed the indigenous language. The written form was in Brahmi, also known as Asokan script. This writing can still be seen on preserved stone inscriptions. With the arrival of Buddhism in the third century B.C., Prakrit came under the influence of Pali.

The Sinhala that is used today is more than 20 centuries old. It has 56 curved and artistically complicated letters. The spoken and written forms of the language are somewhat different, though there have been attempts to make written Sinhala less formal. There are also Sinhala dialects. Sinhala spoken by Sri Lankans in Kandy in the hill country is different from that spoken on the island's coast, both in intonation and in the words used.

ENGLISH

Sri Lankans have colored their spoken English with direct translations of Sinhala expressions, such as "I'll go and come" and "what for the telling," that English speakers elsewhere would have difficulty understanding. Journalists and writers, however, stay closer to the standard English used in the United Kingdom.

This shop sign in Kandy advertises repairs for a number of items including bicycles and watches.

STATUS REVEALED BY FORM OF ADDRESS

In spoken Sinhala specific forms of address indicate the relationship between the person speaking and the person being addressed. For example, the word "you" has several nuances.

Mé or *Oi* ("may" or "oh-ee") is used to attract a person's attention.

Numbe ("NOOM-beh") is formal and used among equals.

Oya ("OH-yeh") is informal and used among friends.

Thamunnaansé ("tha-MOON-NAHN-say") is used to address a superior, monk, VIP, or other respected person. Politicians directly address their audiences with this word.

Thamusé ("tha-MOO-say") is a less polite "you" that carries nuances of derision and annoyance.

Tho ("THOH") is very derogatory. It is used when addressing a person of very low caste or when in the vilest of moods.

Umba ("OOM-beh") is used to address menials and servants. Parents also address their children with this word, as it connotes closeness. Domestic helpers resent the word, but those in ancestral homes would be amazed if addressed otherwise.

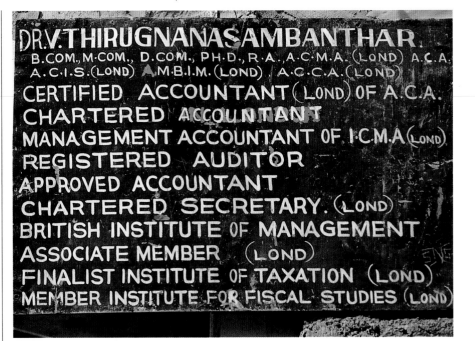

TAMIL

While Sinhala is spoken only in Sri Lanka, Tamil is used by people in other countries as well. It is spoken in the South Indian state of Tamil Nadu, Sri Lanka's closest neighbor in India, as well as in several other Asian countries, such as Malaysia and Singapore, where there are populations of South Indian origin.

ARABIC

For Muslims, whether Moor or Malay, Arabic is the language of religious instruction and prayer. The Moors generally speak Tamil and usually opt to be educated in Tamil. The Malays retain their mother tongue, Malay. Many Malay students choose Sinhala as their medium of instruction, as Malay is not used in school.

BODY LANGUAGE

Sri Lankans are restrained in their hand gestures. This is very evident in movies and television dramas. Even singers stand almost immobile. To compensate, facial expressions exaggerate even subtle feelings. But when it comes to love, gestures and movement play a big role in conveying the message: glances are exchanged, bodies draw near. In formula movies, the hero and heroine in love break into a spirited romp in the bushes, across ponds, and down inclines! Here are other nonverbal signals Sri Lankans use:

GREETING Salutation is dignified. The traditional way is to *namaste* ("neh-MEHS-tay")—bring the palms together at chest level and bend slightly from the waist. People greet a parent, teacher, or religious person by going down on the knees and bending forward right down to the floor with palms together in the *namaste* position.

HEAD WOGGLE To say yes, the head moves from side to side with a down-up, not a sharp left-right, movement. Indians have a similar head gesture signifying agreement.

HAND HOLDING Sri Lankans hold hands when they walk with friends. The sight of two grown men or women walking thus entwined in Sri Lanka does not surprise observers or suggest sexual intimacy.

SITTING It is rude to sit on a higher seat than an elder or better, or with legs stretched out pointing to a shrine or monk. Legs are neatly tucked away.

WALKING It used to be the norm for men to walk, swinging their arms freely, while their wives followed respectfully, carrying baby and baggage. Today, in villages and towns, many women still walk behind, but are no longer beasts of burden. Servants never walk abreast of their employers.

ARTS

THE PAINTINGS AND CRAFTS of Sri Lanka are a kaleidoscope of color and intricacy, of styles and forms. They employ a mixture of tradition and innovation. Some of them have a religious and often ritualistic foundation, used with dance and song to celebrate sacred events.

The professionals of Sri Lanka's traditional arts scene were caste-based. This means that dancers were of one caste, jewelers of another, pottery-makers of a third, and so on. For instance, drummers came from the *berawaya* ("bear-ah-WAH-yah") caste, and no other caste took to drumming as a means of livelihood or even as a pastime. The castes to which artistes belonged were below the farmers and the aristocracy.

This has changed now with the existence of colleges and youth centers that emphasize the arts. Traditional arts, which would have faded away if they had been left to be passed on from generation to generation, are thus enjoying a revival with young Sri Lankans.

The freedom for anyone to practice the arts has eliminated a monopoly on the arts or on any one art form by caste or dynasty. Art is also being promoted by the government and by private enterprise through the sponsorship of exhibitions abroad.

Opposite: **Wooden masks worn by dancers in Ambalangoda, a center of mask-making.**

Below: **The majestic elephant, a protected species in Sri Lanka, is featured in much of the country's historical art. Sri Lankans believe elephants have a caste system. This elephant's tusks and posture show that it belongs to a high caste.**

A Kandyan dancer strikes a trance-like pose. In earlier times, only senior dancers wore the headdress. Now, however, many school children wear it after their apprenticeship under a trained teacher.

DANCE

There are two Sinhalese dance styles: low country and hill country. Low-country dance combines elements of mime, dramatic dialogue, and impersonation, and the dancers often wear strange and scary masks.

Performed in the coastal belt south of Colombo, low-country dancing usually features exorcism. For example, the devil dance, which may last 12 hours, weaves together humor and frightening images to heal the sick. Exorcism is a carefully crafted ritual that originated in Sri Lanka's pre-Buddhist era. It incorporates ancient Ayurvedic ideas about the causes of disease. The frightening demon mask worn by the devil dancer is believed to be both the cause of and the cure for the illness. In the *bali* ("BAH-li") dance, the dancer talks to the evil spirit that has possessed the sick person to draw out the spirit and chase it away.

Both low-country and hill-country styles use vigorous movements and traditional costumes. Hill-country dances have classical origins and have been passed down in traditional Kandyan dancing families from father to son for many generations. The Kandyan dancer wears yards of frilly white, red-trimmed cloth, a beaded breastplate, and an intricate silver headdress. Bells around his ankles jingle, as the dancer pirouettes, skips, whirls, and stamps his feet to the rhythm of the drums. Kandyan dance involves a lot of acrobatic cartwheels and leaps. The *vannama* ("veh-NAH-meh") imitates the movements of animals. Watching the *gajaba* ("geh-JAH-beh") *vannama*, for instance, one can clearly see the movements of a majestic elephant.

The Tamils retain Indian classical dances such as *bharatanatyam*. The Burghers prefer Western dances such as ballroom styles and ballet. The *kaffringa* and *baila* dance styles introduced by the Portuguese are popular at parties, and even five-star hotels have *baila* sessions.

THE BEAT OF THE DRUM

The usual Sri Lankan musical ensemble includes drums with tiny cymbals and a conch shell or horn pipe called *horaneva* ("HOR-ah-NAY-vah"). Cylindrical or conical drums, *bera* ("BAY-rah"), have wooden frames with animal skins stretched over the opening. They are tapped with the fingers and palm or else beaten with a cane stick. Some common drums are the *geta* ("get-teh") *bera*, *devale* ("DAY-vah-leh") *bera*, and *yak* ("yuk") *bera* used in devil-dancing.

Urban Sri Lankans enjoy Western music. Orchestras play classical music. Jazz has not caught on much. Several musicians popular in Sri Lanka and abroad sing Sinhalese and Tamil songs.

A village drum team.

THEATER

Four varieties of Sri Lankan folk drama have evolved. The *sokari* ("sew-KAH-ri") is an adaptation of rituals once performed for an abundant harvest. In the almost extinct *nadagam* ("NAH-deh-gum") and *kavi* ("KAH-vi") *nagadam* from Ambalangoda, a narrator relates the story as masked dancers portray the characters. The fourth variety, *kolam* ("KOH-lum"), is an all-night event.

Contemporary theater is alive in all three languages, but predominantly in Sinhala. Local English-language productions range from original drama to Shakespeare to spectacular musicals like *Les Miserables*.

Sri Lankans get to watch films in English, Tamil, and Hindi. Since Lester James Peiris' *Rekawa* in the 1950s, quality Sinhala films have also been screened in Sri Lankan movie theaters. In patronage of the arts, the government has renovated and refurbished an old theater—the Tower Hall—and a cinema hall—the Elphinstone.

The work of craftsmen decorates a temple on the southern coast.

Decorated lacquer canisters.

CRAFTS

MASK MAKING This folk art originated in Ambalangoda, south of Colombo. Devil-dance masks are carved from wood and painted in shocking colors. They come in various sizes, depending on their use: the souvenirs are small, while those for ceremonies fit the head and those for ornaments are oversized. Used in dance, the ritual masks have a hypnotic effect. Collectors see them as artistic masterpieces. Each mask has the face of a particular demon that represents a specific mental or physical illness commonly experienced by the villagers. The identities of the 18 or so core demons differ from area to area, or even across communities in one area.

WOOD AND IVORY CARVING The ancient craft of woodcarving is still actively practiced, mostly by artisans in the Kandy area. Their delicate filigree panels decorate the tops of doors, windows, and tables. Ivory elephants—with filigree-worked, gem-encrusted gold or silver coverings, depicting *perahera* ("PAIR-ah-HAIR-ah"), or festival, elephants—testify to the talent and dedication of professional artisans.

STONE SCULPTING This craft was practiced while the ancient royal capitals were at Anuradhapura and Polonnaruwa and the kings were patrons of the arts. There are gigantic, well-proportioned rock statues in both places. It is believed that the magnificent Aukana Buddha, 36 feet (11 m) tall, was built by King Dhatusena in the fifth century A.D. More impressive, though smaller, the Samadhi Pilame, or Meditative Statue, in Anuradhapura greatly inspired the first Indian prime minister, Jawarharlal Nehru. Isurumuniya, also in Anuradhapura, is a picturesque temple with a quiet pool, with two exquisite carvings, one of a rider on a horse, the other of two lovers.

METALWORK AND POTTERY The island has a long tradition of metalwork using gold, silver, copper, tin, and alloys such as bronze. A traditional Tamil wedding custom involves the groom tying a gold wedding necklace, called a *thali*, around the bride's neck. The Kandyan bride is required to wear seven items of jewelry around her neck.

Pottery is a living craft, practiced in homes and temples. Every household has a pitcher or big-bellied clay pot to store water. Temples have clay oil lamps, and clay vessels were traditionally used for cooking.

MATS AND BASKETS Mats adorn every rural home and some urban houses, particularly Buddhist ones. Kalutara, a town south of Colombo, displays mats and handicrafts in wayside shops. In the Dumbara valley, close to Kandy, is a village where hempen weaving is an exquisite art.

The island is rich in material for baskets of rattan, bamboo, rush, and palm leaves. Jaffna baskets, justly famous, are made from palmyra leaves and are reputed to be able to hold water. Many kitchens have containers, strainers, food covers, and carpets made of natural products, including coconut coir.

A brass effigy of the war god Skanda. Effigies like this are sold at a souvenir kiosk near the Skanda shrine at Kataragama.

LEISURE

THERE IS A LOT OF TIME for leisure in Sri Lanka. School lasts only from 8 A.M. to 2 P.M., after which children can hang out and play. Working adults pursue recreational activities after office hours and on weekends. In addition, there are 24 public holidays. Many women, however, have to juggle household chores, childcare, and paid jobs.

Evenings are a popular time for jogging, strolling, swimming, and fishing. The elite, especially in Colombo, play tennis and squash and patronize gymnasiums and health centers. Other Sri Lankans play team sports on the village green or enjoy competitive cycling.

TRADITIONAL GAMES

Games handed down through generations are played mostly during the April New Year season and at national festivals. A favorite game involves trying to climb a greased pole to retrieve a flag attached to the top. Pillow fights never fail to amuse onlookers. They are fun, and one does not need skill to play. Two players sit astride a pole, with one hand behind their backs, and swipe at each other with a pillow in the other hand. The one who sends the opponent tumbling off the pole wins the game.

Women prefer indoor games, though men do enjoy card games and throwing dice, betting being the whole fun. A favorite indoor game is *panche* ("PUNCH-eh"), similar to Parcheesi. Instead of dice, *panche* uses seven shells. With the first throw, the shells rest belly down on the ground. Points are earned by moving a marker around the board toward "home." In *olinda kelina* ("oh-LIN-dah KAY-li-nah"), each player moves red seeds on a low bench with two rows of holes. The aim is to "eat" the opponent's seeds. The first player to deposit all his or her seeds safely in the large hole at one end of the bench wins.

Opposite: **A friendly cricket game at Weligama. Cricket is the national sport of Sri Lanka.**

Windsurfing and other water sports are popular in the island's many natural bays.

SPORTS

Sri Lankans are very conscious of the link between health and physical recreation. Social clubs, youth centers, and schools spend a lot of money on developing sports for children and young people, while track-and-field sports get state funding.

Cycling is popular. Races are often held on public highways, and non-participants run the risk of getting doused with buckets of water meant to cool the cyclists. Tennis and golf have a long history in the country. Soccer is played year round. The rugby season runs from April to August.

During cricket season, from January to March, there are the annual interschool cricket matches, such as the Battle of the Blues between the Royal College and St. Thomas' College. Sri Lanka became a full member of the International Cricket Foundation in 1982, and the Sri Lanka team won the 1996 World Cup in England.

Sri Lanka has her star athletes too. Muttiah Muralitharan is one of the top off-spinners in international cricket. Thuhashini Selvaratnam entered

the Guinness Book of World Records in 1989 as the youngest person to hold a golf championship title. She was 12.

In 2000, "wonder girl" Susanthika Jayasinghe became the first Sri Lankan woman to win an Olympic medal. She barely missed the silver in the finals of the 200-m sprint in Sydney and took the bronze instead. Sri Lanka has also fared well in the Asian and South Asian Games and in the Davis Cup tennis tournament.

READING AND TELEVISION

Sri Lanka has a 91 percent literacy rate, among the highest in Asia. As everyone is interested in political events, reading is the most popular indoor leisure activity. Public library membership is high, and publishing journals and comic books in Sinhala and Tamil is a lucrative business. For the couch potatoes, there are several television channels: Rupavahini, the Independent Television Network (ITN), TNL, and ETV, besides the cable channels.

Enjoying the sea breeze at Galle Face Green, a field facing the sea at Colombo.

FESTIVALS

SRI LANKANS CELEBRATE so many festivals that their year is filled with public holidays. Religious festivals are definite holidays, and each of the four main religious groups—Buddhists, Hindus, Christians, and Muslims —celebrate at least two annual festivals. In addition, there are holidays declared for national anniversaries and monthly full-moon *poya* days observed by the Buddhists. On average, Sri Lankans enjoy almost a month's worth of public holidays each year.

Festivals in Sri Lanka are a cocktail of noise and color. Most have a streak of religious and national fervor. At Vesak, Buddhists brighten their homes and temples with coconut-oil lamps. A religious festival may be enjoyed even by those who do not profess the particular faith. Christmas, for example, is a time of feasting and merrymaking for all.

Opposite: **A Kandyan dance performance at the Perahera Festival.**

SRI LANKA'S FESTIVE CALENDAR

Here is a glimpse of Sri Lanka's calendar of festivals:

Buddhists observe the *poya* day every month. However, the five major full-moon days are Duruthu in January, Vesak in May, Poson in June, Esala in August, and Unduvap in December.

The big Hindu festivals are Thai Pongal in January, Maha Sivarathri in February/March, Vel in July/August, and Deepavali in October/November.

The Muslim festivals of Ramadan, Haj, and Milad-un-Nabi, the birthday of the prophet Mohammed, are celebrated in different months in different years, according to the lunar calendar.

Christians in Sri Lanka, as elsewhere, celebrate Christmas in December and Good Friday and Easter in March/April.

In addition, Sri Lanka celebrates the following national holidays: Independence Day on February 4 and May Day on May 1. The Sinhalese and Tamil New Year falls in April.

> "Away from the clamor of the city, it is easier to appreciate the gentle, timeless nature of the festival [Vesak]. The illuminations are different here. Every tiny garden glows with the light of simple paper lanterns, each containing one flickering candle. Doorsteps and verandahs are lined with tiny coconut-oil lamps made of clay ... the row of minute, yellow flames creates an effect utterly out of proportion to the simplicity with which it is achieved."
>
> —Richard Simon, in Sri Lanka: The Resplendent Isle

BUDDHIST FESTIVALS

Vesak, the full-moon day in May, commemorates the birth, enlightenment, and death of Siddhartha Gautama, the Buddha. Vesak is essentially a religious festival, austere and devotional more than merry and joyous. Buddhists go to the temple and give the day to worship. Many observe the eight or 10 precepts, three or five more than the basic daily requirement, and spend a good part of the day and night in meditation.

Vesak takes on a festive quality after dark. Every home, office, and public place is decorated with strings of lightbulbs, candle-lit paper lanterns, or earthen oil lamps. In the big cities people throng the streets to admire the lights. Open-air theaters attract crowds. The main draw, though, is the *pandal* ("PAN-doll").

The *pandal* is a large wooden structure, 60 to 70 feet (18 to 21 m) tall, with painted panels depicting a Jataka tale or a story from the life of the Buddha. The panels are rimmed with rows of little multicolored lights, which blink according to a set pattern. A very large *pandal* uses up to 50,000 bulbs. Music blares forth until the story of the *pandal* is related, also very loudly. Several *dansela* ("DHUN-seh-leh"), or temporary eating houses, offer free food and soft drinks to passers-by.

The *pandal* and *dansela* are funded from collections made throughout the year. Even the poorest tradesman will donate a few rupees, for no one begrudges contributing money toward this important festival. There is no *pandal* in rural areas; Vesak celebrations there are quiet but charming.

Poson, also a major *poya* day, commemorates the introduction of Buddhism in Sri Lanka. Poson falls on the full-moon day in June, when devotees hold processions all over the country, but especially at Anuradhapura and Mihintale, where Mahinda met King Devanampiya Tissa and preached his first Buddhist sermon.

There are three more major full-moon days: Duruthu, Esala, and Unduvap. The other *poya* days, one every month, are celebrated with national as well as religious fervor, though they are essentially days for meditation, simple living, and generous giving.

The lights of the *pandal* draw attention to the panels that tell the Buddha's story.

PERAHERA

In 1775 monks came from Siam (now Thailand) to restore discipline in
monasteries in Sri Lanka. While in Kandy, they saw the Esala festival,
during which Hindus ask the island's four guardian deities, or *devale*, for
protection. The monks protested that Hindu practices were so strong in
a country where Buddhism was the established religion. To please the
monks, the king of Kandy ordered that the tooth relic of the Buddha be
paraded ahead of the *devale*. Thus was born Sri Lanka's most spectacular
festival, Kandy's Esala Perahera.

The Esala Perahera lasts two weeks in July/August. For five nights,
dancers, tom-tom beaters, torch bearers, acrobats, and decorated elephants
walk in processions in the precincts of the four *devale*—Kataragama,
Natha, Vishnu, and Pattini. More elephants join each night, adding color
and grandeur to the procession.

On the sixth night, the festival ventures beyond the *devale* precincts.
A magnificent temple elephant bearing a howdah that holds a replica of
the tooth relic enters the procession, followed by the chief trustee and
other officials of the Dalada Maligawa, or Temple of the Tooth, all dressed
in traditional Kandyan court attire.

The seventh night introduces six palanquins carrying ancient jewelry
and weapons. Palanquins used to be a mode of travel for women of the
aristocracy. The palanquin procession lasts five nights.

The Esala Perahera ends with a water-cutting ceremony. The sword of
the Kataragama deity is used to "cut" a circle in the water of a river just
outside Kandy. Four earthen pots are filled with water from within the
circle. The tooth relic is brought back to the Dalada Maligawa, and each
devale procession returns to its precinct, bringing along one of the four
pots of water, to be kept until the next Esala Perahera.

The day procession of the Esala Perahera. A replica of the Tooth Relic casket is carried on the back of the majestic Maligawa elephant.

HINDU FESTIVALS

Most Hindu festivals are celebrated in temples. Besides Thai Pongal, a harvest festival, and Deepavali, the festival of lights, Hindus celebrate several other festivals. The most spectacular is the festival at Kataragama in the south of the island. During this festival in July, many Hindus do penance by passing skewers through their tongue and cheeks, pulling carts attached to hooks in their backs, and balancing on their shoulders a *kavadi*, a semicircular frame covered with red paper and peacock feathers.

A Hindu at Kataragama prepares for sacrifice.

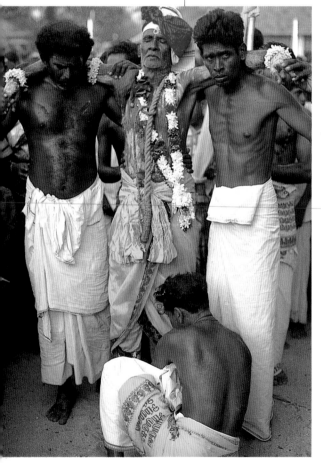

A procession takes the head priest bearing the *yantra* ("YUN-tra"), or relic of the god, to the Valli Amma temple. After a few days, the *yantra* is returned to the main Kataragama temple.

The highlight of the Kataragama festival is an awe-inspiring firewalking ceremony. Many Hindu devotees take it as their sacred duty to walk over burning coals to appease the warrior god Skanda. People from all parts of the country, indeed people from other countries, visit Kataragama during the festival to see the firewalkers.

After bathing in the Menik Ganga, or River of Gems, devotees meditate and ask the gods to bless them. They then walk or run across a bed of burning coals, the heat of which can be felt yards away. The firewalkers are believed to be in a special state of mind, as they are able to walk on the coals without getting their soles blistered or burned.

Buddhists also celebrate the Kataragama festival. They pray at the Kiri Vihara temple, then offer flowers and prayers to the god Skanda and smash open a coconut on the ground.

A month or two after the Kataragama festival, the Vel festival is held in Colombo to celebrate the marriage of the god Skanda to his queen, Deivanai. The main streets of Colombo take on a carnival atmosphere during this festival. A beautifully decorated chariot, accompanied by priests and a crowd of devotees, travels a distance of about 6 miles (9.7 km) from the Sea Street temple in Pettah, Colombo's bazaar area, to a temple in Bambalapitiya. The chariot stops frequently to be piled with flowers and other offerings and for people lining the streets to be blessed. Vel is a festive time for everyone in the city. Vendors crowd the streets, offering multicolored bangles, bead necklaces, and bric-a-brac for sale.

During the festival at Udappuwa, Hindu devotees carry offerings to the god Ganapati, who blesses new endeavors.

CHRISTIAN FESTIVALS

Santa Claus, fruitcake, wine, carols, and trees covered in bows and lights mark the season of Christmas in Sri Lanka, much as they do in other countries. But to Christians, the true spirit of Christmas is sharing. In 2000, a Catholic priest in Sri Lanka encouraged Catholic families to take young war victims at a Buddhist orphanage into their homes on Christmas Day. The response was enthusiastic, some families even asking to have their guest for the whole season.

MUSLIM FESTIVALS

Muslim festivals that are publicly celebrated are Milad-un-Nabi—the prophet Mohammed's birthday—and the feast day that ends the fast in the month of Ramadan. *Vatalappan* ("VAHT-leh-up-pun"), a sweet steamed pudding, and *biryani* ("bir-YAH-n,"), an aromatic spicy rice with lamb or chicken, are prepared, and Muslim families share a meal with their non-Muslim friends. Galle Face Green in the heart of Colombo is the site of a mass gathering of Muslim men praying on these festival days.

NEW YEAR

Both Aluth Avuruddha, the Sinhalese new year, and the Hindu new year are celebrated in April to mark the sun's entry into the constellation of Aries. They are also harvest festivals, when the major crop is gathered.

Traditions are followed closely. An astrologer dictates the time for all activities. The old year ends at a particular time, when all hearths have to be extinguished. The new year begins at a prescribed auspicious time, and the hearth is lit again. During the in-between period, the *nonagathe* ("non-ah-GAH-thay"), no work is to be done. The astrologer advises on what to cook for the first meal (milk rice is the usual main dish), what color the chief female householder should wear, and which direction she should face as she strikes the first match to light the hearth.

Aluth Avuruddha is a time for family closeness, showing respect to elders, gift-giving, feasting, drinking, and playing games. New clothes and furnishings, and even new pots and pans are bought. Swings on trees and giant wheels appear on village threshing fields. Elephant races are held; children start pillow fights. Women play the *rabana* ("RAH-bah-neh"): they sit around a circular drum with a fire lit underneath and beat the drum in unison.

OTHER CELEBRATIONS

Independence Day is celebrated with parades, dances, and national games. The president raises the national flag opposite the parliament building in Sri Jayewardenepura or at Independence Square, and there is a parade of the armed forces.

On May Day, streets and parks become seas of green, red, blue, and purple—the colors of political parties holding rallies.

FOOD

THE MOUTHWATERING AROMAS of the food from the "spice island" can work up anyone's appetite. Sri Lankan curries are loaded with spices, such as tamarind, turmeric, cardamom, cinnamon, coriander, and lemon grass. Chili pepper—whether green or red, chopped or ground or roasted and powdered, fresh or dried—finds its way into almost any dish. Traditional housewives roast and grind their own spice blends rather than buy ready-packed spices off shop shelves—they claim the latter are not fresh.

RICE AND CURRY

The staple food is rice, eaten with curry. Two other staples are hoppers and stringhoppers, similar to pancakes, the latter resembling a circular pancake of netted dough strings. Urbanites have bread for breakfast, with eggs and fruit. On weekends, they may laze over a more traditional breakfast consisting of milk rice and stringhoppers, with *katta sambol* ("kut-teh SUM-bole"), made of ground red chilies, onions, Maldive fish, and lime.

The dinner staple could be rice, string-hoppers, hoppers, or a local pancake-like bread called *roti* ("ROH-ti"). There will be at least four curries and one or two side dishes. The meal is not complete without *badung* ("BAH-doong"), fried dried fish; vegetables with lentils; *malung* ("MEHL-loong"), finely-shredded leaves cooked lightly or served raw; and *papadam* ("PAH-peh-doom"), a puffy, crisp, spicy wafer.

Opposite: **A taste of Sri Lankan cuisine.**

Below: **Buyers and sellers bargain at the market over food prices.**

125

Trucks unload bunches of king coconut, the juice of which may be drunk plain or with lime or a pinch of salt.

DRINK

Tea is the most widely drunk beverage in Sri Lanka. The country's finest teas are produced from crops grown above 3,500 feet (1,067 m). Sri Lankans take their tea plain or sweetened, with milk or with a slice of lemon. A popular local version is tea brewed with ginger.

Two other favorite drinks, *tambili* ("TAM-biee-lee") and *kurumba* ("koo-ROOM-bah"), are believed to be good for the health. *Tambili* is the water of the orange-hued young coconut; *kurumba* is the water from green coconuts. Cordials are made from many varieties of Sri Lankan fruit—oranges, grapefruit, mangoes, and especially passion fruit. Bottled water and soft drinks are widely available.

Two alcoholic beverages are derived from the coconut palm. Toddy is the fermented sap, and *arrack* ("AIR-rack") is distilled from toddy. The sap of the *kitul* ("KI-tool") palm inflorescence yields a sweet toddy rich in vitamins. The tax on *arrack* keeps increasing, encouraging illicit brews. *Kassippu* ("kah-see-poo") is a potent illicit brew.

A TUTTI-FRUTTI INDUSTRY

Sri Lanka's food-processing industry has been innovative, using the country's wealth of tropical fruit to produce fruit pickles and chutneys, fruit cordials and syrups, fruit jams and marmalades, and dehydrated and canned fruit for both domestic consumption and export. Small-scale enterprises have expanded with the help of the Sri Lanka Agribusiness-Enterprise Project, funded by the United States Agency for International Development.

In 1999 Lanka Canneries Limited, a fruit- and vegetable-processing company in Colombo, introduced low-sugar fruit jams to the Sri Lankan market. The healthy jams contain 20 percent less sugar, but 20 percent more fruit—passion fruit, pineapple, woodapple, and mango—to meet the demand from an increasingly health-conscious Sri Lankan public.

Mahaweli Canneries, a jam and cordial company west of Colombo, has created a colorful fruit topping for ice cream, cakes, and other desserts. Unripe papayas are first soaked in a sugar solution, then diced. Different-colored food dyes are added to separate batches of the diced papaya. The stained papaya pieces are next placed in a gas-powered dryer.

The dried pieces of different colors are finally mixed and packed for sale. The company has expanded to produce dehydrated jackfruit and breadfruit as well.

A mobile drinks seller helps quench the thirst of vacationers at Galle.

FRUIT

Sri Lanka is a tropical fruit paradise, with varieties to please every taste. Durian, the "king of fruit," is irresistible to some, but repugnant to others with its "rotten" smell, which carries for quite a distance. Mango varieties come in different colors, sizes, and flavors. The color of banana peels may be green, yellow, or reddish-brown. Plantain, a large banana with starchy flesh, is sliced and fried. Pineapple is sometimes added to salads to add piquancy. Woodapples and passion fruit are used to make jams. Pawpaw, or papaya, is considered a health food.

A store at the old Galle market sells *mee kiri* ("MEE kee-ree"), made of thick milk yogurt mixed with thick, dark honey.

TABLE MANNERS

The traditional way to eat rice and curry is to use the fingers of the right hand to shape little portions of the rice and curry into small balls that can be easily popped into the mouth. It is believed that a Sri Lankan meal tastes better when the diner uses the fingers instead of a fork and spoon. Eating with the fingers is not messy if managed correctly. Properly handled, the food should touch only the fingertips and not get stuck on the lips or beard.

Villagers often use earthenware vessels as plates and sometimes drink out of polished coconut shells. Ceramic plates and cups, however, are fast replacing traditional utensils. Traditional meals are eaten from leaf mats on the floor. Urbanites sit at the dining table, the focus of social activity in many homes. At mealtimes the mother usually dishes out the plates of rice. She may then add the curries as well or leave them in separate containers on the table.

FOOD BELIEFS

Sri Lankans have several food taboos. Hindus consider the cow sacred and do not eat beef; many are also vegetarians. Buddhists also avoid eating beef, and Muslims do not eat pork or the meat of animals that have not been slaughtered the Islamic way.

Sinhalese and Tamils believe that some foods are "heaty," while others are "cooling." They say that someone who eats shellfish or "bloodfish," breadfruit, or yellow tuna, for example, may get a redness in the eye. One cools the body by drinking plenty of barley water. There is no clear explanation, however, as to why ice water is considered heaty!

Someone who comes down with chicken pox, mumps, or measles is not allowed to eat any animal product. Instead the patient gets bland meals consisting of rice and vegetables cooked without chili or saffron.

Food served in a Hindu temple hall is always vegetarian.

EATING OUT

Dining out is a family treat. The poor have their *buth kadé* ("BOOTH keh-day"), or rice shop. In villages, there is the *kopi kadé* ("KOH-pee keh-day"), or coffeeshop, which is more a social club. On the street, one can look for vendors selling *godamba roti* ("GO-dum-ber ROH-ti"), a paper-thin, square pancake with or without egg.

People in Colombo can dine at restaurants serving Chinese, Japanese, Korean, Thai, French, Swiss, German, and Indian food, in addition to local cuisine. Besides Western fast-food outlets, such as McDonald's and Pizza Hut, there is also the Indian version, Komala's.

YELLOW RICE

3 cups (710 ml) long grain rice
4 tablespoons butter
2 finely-sliced medium onions
6 whole cloves
20 black peppercorns
3½ teaspoons salt
1½ teaspoons ground turmeric
5 cups (1.2 l) coconut milk

Wash rice and drain thoroughly. Heat butter in a saucepan. Add onions and fry until golden brown. Add cloves, peppercorns, salt, and turmeric. Add rice and fry, stirring constantly, until rice is well coated with butter and turmeric. Add coconut milk and bring to a boil. Reduce heat, cover with lid, and cook for another 25 minutes or so, without lifting the lid. When rice is cooked, the spices used will have surfaced to the top. Remove the spices and serve the rice hot with curry.

SRI LANKAN VEGETABLE CURRY

3 medium finely-chopped green chilies
1 medium finely-chopped onion
½ teaspoon turmeric
1 stick cinnamon
3 cloves finely-chopped garlic
1 teaspoon finely-chopped ginger

1 teaspoon lemongrass
3 cups coconut milk
2 cups water
Salt to taste
4 cups sliced vegetables (cabbage, potatoes, zucchini, yellow squash, tomatoes)

In a soup pot, combine chilies, onion, turmeric, cinnamon, garlic, ginger, lemongrass, one cup coconut milk, water, and salt. Simmer for 10 minutes: Add vegetables and cook until tender. Add remaining coconut milk. Simmer for five minutes. Serve with rice.

SRI LANKAN SPICY EGGPLANT

4 eggplants
Oil for frying
2.6 ounces (75 g) chopped onion

1 chopped fresh chili
½ teaspoon salt
Juice of 1 lime

Wash and dice eggplants. Heat oil and fry eggplant until browned. Remove and drain excess oil, then place in a dish. Add onion, chili, salt, and lime juice. Mix well. Serve with rice.

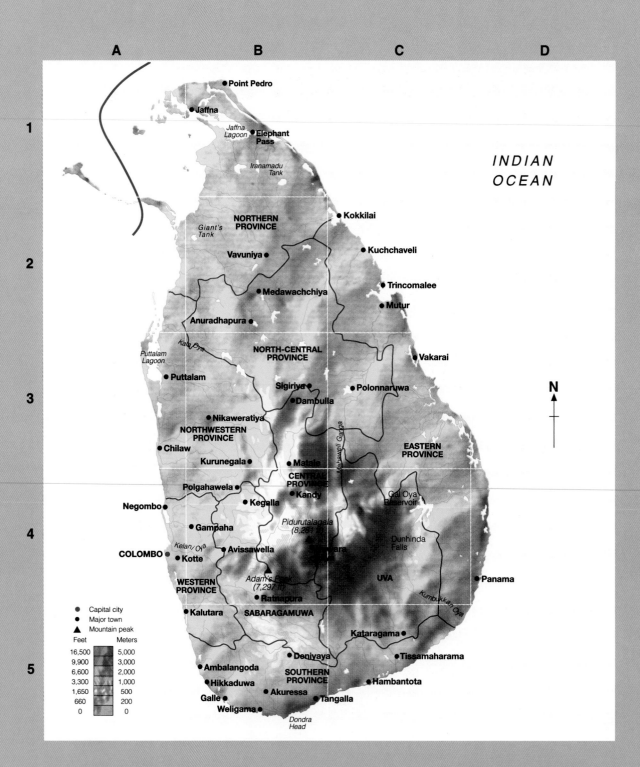

MAP OF SRI LANKA

ECONOMIC SRI LANKA

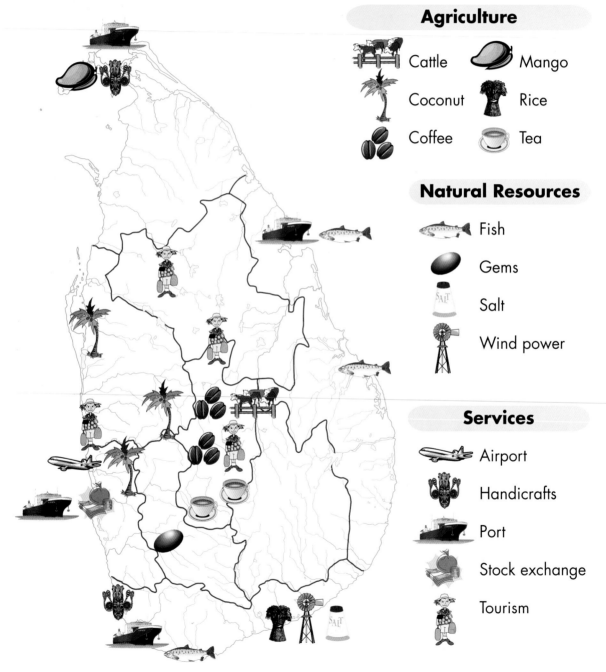

Agriculture

- Cattle
- Mango
- Coconut
- Rice
- Coffee
- Tea

Natural Resources

- Fish
- Gems
- Salt
- Wind power

Services

- Airport
- Handicrafts
- Port
- Stock exchange
- Tourism

ABOUT THE ECONOMY

OVERVIEW
Sri Lanka's economy has been badly affected by an 18-year civil war. Mainly agricultural, the country also has some industry, especially garment manufacturing for export. Tea is a major foreign exchange earner. Sri Lankans unable to find work at home migrate to other Asian countries to work as domestic helpers and on construction sites. Migrant labor is the second highest foreign income earner. Tourism is an important industry, but it has its ups and downs, in large part due to terrorism activities carried out by the Liberation Tigers of Tamil Eelam. Hydroelectricity is the country's main source of power, though there are projects in alternative sources of power such as solar and wind energy.

GROSS DOMESTIC PRODUCT
$62.7 billion (2000)

LAND USE
Forest and woodland 32 percent, cultivated land 29 percent, pasture 7 percent, other 32 percent

CURRENCY
1 Sri Lankan rupee (LKR) = 100 cents
Notes: 10, 20, 50, 100, 200, 1000 rupees
Coins: 5, 10, 25, 50 cents; 1, 2, 5, 10 rupees
USD 1 = LKR 95.35 (March 2002)

AGRICULTURAL PRODUCTS
Rice, vegetables, fruit, sugarcane, coconut, dairy products, fish, and meat

WORKFORCE
6,673,000 (1999)

UNEMPLOYMENT RATE
8.9 percent (1999)

MAJOR EXPORTS
Tea, garments, rubber, gems

MAJOR IMPORTS
Food items, medicines, machinery and equipment, raw materials, mineral fuels, chemicals

MAJOR TRADING PARTNERS
India, Pakistan, China, United States of America, Great Britain

MAJOR PORTS
Sea ports at Colombo, Galle, Trincomalee (natural harbor); Katunayake International Airport

MAJOR AID DONORS
Japan, United States of America, China

INTERNATIONAL PARTICIPATION
Commonwealth of Nations; Non-Aligned Movement (NAM); South Asian Association for Regional Cooperation (SAARC); United Nations Educational, Scientific, and Cultural Organization (UNESCO); World Intellectual Property Organization (WIPO)

CULTURAL SRI LANKA

Holy City
The remains of the ancient city of Anuradhapura are visited by Buddhist pilgrims every year. The city was built around a fig tree started from a cutting from the tree under which the Buddha attained enlightenment. The oldest temple here is believed to house the Buddha's right collar-bone. Anuradhapura, with its ancient temples and palaces, has been declared a World Heritage Site by UNESCO.

Esala Perahera
Kandy is the home of the Temple of the Tooth, which houses the sacred Tooth Relic of the Buddha. Pilgrims visit the relic everyday, amid drumming and chanting. During the Esala Perahera, a festival in July/August, an elephant carries a casket containing a replica of the sacred tooth through the streets in a colorful parade of decorated elephants, drummers, and dancers.

Elephant Orphanage
The Pinnawela Elephant Orphanage was set up by the government as a home for baby elephants found in the wild with no mother. The elephants can roam freely in the orphanage, and keepers bathe and feed them at regular times.

City of Gems
Ratnapura is the center of Sri Lanka's gem industry. Rubies, sapphires, topaz, amethysts, aquamarines, garnets, zircons, and other gems are mined, cut, and polished in Ratnapura and exported to countries around the world.

Sinharaja Forest Reserve
The only remaining expanse of virgin tropical rain forest in the Sri Lankan lowlands, the Sinharaja forest is home to many endemic species of plants and animals. The forest was declared a biosphere reserve in 1978 and a Natural World Heritage Site in 1988.

Old Dutch Fort
At the old Dutch fort in Galle are Dutch houses, museums, churches, and the New Oriental Hotel, built for Dutch governors in 1684.

Uda Walawe National Park
This park was established to protect the Uda Walawe reservoir and to provide a new home for animals displaced by the Walawe River Development Scheme. The park has elephants, wildcats, fox, bears, monkeys, wild pigs, leopards, spotted deer, snakes, butterflies, and birds such as the rare red-faced malkoha.

Swami Rock
Trincomalee is the site of a huge rock known as Swami Rock, on which lie the ruins of the ancient Temple of a Thousand Columns. The temple was the largest of at least three built on the rock by Hindus, but it was destroyed in 1624 by the Portuguese, who built a fort in its place. Both Hindus and Buddhists today venerate this site, bringing fruit and flower offerings every year.

Lion Mountain
Sigiriya is an ancient city with water and boulder gardens and cave paintings. At the top of Lion Mountain—a rock rising 656 feet (200 m)—are the remains of an old fortress.

Dunhinda Falls
One of Sri Lanka's most beautiful waterfalls, though not one of its tallest, the Dunhinda gets its name from the mist it creates (dun means "mist") as the water falls from a height of 210 feet (60 m).

Lovers' Leap
Legend has it that two lovers, not allowed to be together, jumped to their death at this waterfall, hence its name. Lovers' Leap begins in the south slope of Pidurutalagala, Sri Lanka's highest mountain, and can be seen from Nuwara Eliya.

ABOUT THE CULTURE

OFFICIAL NAME
The Democratic Socialist Republic of Sri Lanka

CAPITAL
Colombo

GOVERNMENT
Democratic government with executive president and 225-member parliament

DESCRIPTION OF FLAG
On the right-hand side of the Sri Lankan flag is a crimson block with a yellow sword-bearing lion. On the left are two vertical bands, one green, one orange. The flag symbolizes the independence yet unity of the major ethnic groups: the lion represents the Sinhalese, believed to be descended from a lion; the green band represents the Moors; and the orange band represents the Tamils. In the corners of the crimson area are four bo leaves that stand for universal love, kindness, joy, and equanimity.

POPULATION
19,408,635 (2001)

LIFE EXPECTANCY
72 years (male 70, female 75)

LITERACY RATE
91.8 percent (male 92 percent, female 90 percent)

ETHNIC GROUPS
Sinhalese 74 percent, Sri Lankan Tamils 12.7 percent, Moors 7 percent, Indian Tamils 5.5 percent, Others 0.8 percent

RELIGIONS
Buddhism 69.3 percent, Hinduism 15.5 percent, Christianity 7.6 percent, Islam 7.6 percent, Others 0.1 percent

OFFICIAL LANGUAGES
Sinhala and Tamil

NATIONAL HOLIDAYS
Thai Pongal, National Day, Sinhalese and Tamil New Year, Good Friday, Vesak, Poson, Deepavali, Christmas, Milad-un-Nabi, Id-ul-Fitr

LEADERS IN POLITICS
Don Stephen Senanayake—first prime minister
J.R. Jayewardene—first president
Sirimavo R.D. Bandaranaike—world's first woman prime minister

LEADERS IN SPORTS
Muttiah Muralitharan—became world's youngest bowler to take 400 Test wickets in 2002
Susanthika Jayasinghe—bronze medalist in 2000 Olympics 200-m sprint
Arjuna Ranatunge—led cricket team to 1996 World Cup victory
Duncan White—silver medalist in 1958 Olympics hurdles

TIME LINE

IN SRI LANKA	IN THE WORLD
5,000 B.C. Cave dweller Balangoda Man uses fire and develops rudimentary agriculture.	**753 B.C.** Rome is founded.
500 B.C. Arrival of Indo-Aryans, Prince Vijaya and 700 followers	
250 B.C. Buddhism is introduced by Mahinda, the son of Emperor Asoka.	
170 B.C. Dutu Gemunu defeats Elara. Golden Age begins with agricultural development and construction of tanks and stupas.	**116–17 B.C.** The Roman Empire reaches its greatest extent under Emperor Trajan (98-17).
A.D. 455–473 Royal capital moves to Polonnaruwa.	**A.D. 600** Height of Mayan civilization
	1000 The Chinese perfect gunpowder and begin to use it in warfare.
1371 Royal capital moves to Kotte.	
1505 Portuguese arrive.	
1521 Royal capital moves to Sitawaka; Kandyan kingdom gains power.	**1530** Beginning of trans-Atlantic slave trade organized by the Portuguese in Africa.
	1558–1603 Reign of Elizabeth I of England
1606 Dutch arrive.	**1620** Pilgrim Fathers sail the Mayflower to America.
1638 Dutch expel Portuguese.	
	1776 U.S. Declaration of Independence
1796 British East India Company is established.	**1789–99** The French Revolution
1802 Ceylon becomes a British Crown Colony.	
1815 Ceylon is unified under British rule.	

IN SRI LANKA	IN THE WORLD
1847–57	
Coffee plantations thrive.	
1860s	**1861**
Introduction of tea as commercial crop	The U.S. Civil War begins.
	1869
1870s	The Suez Canal is opened.
Introduction of rubber as commercial crop	**1914**
	World War I begins.
1931	
Universal suffrage is granted to men and women over 21 years of age.	**1939**
	World War II begins.
	1945
1948	The United States drops atomic bombs on
Independence from British rule	Hiroshima and Nagasaki.
	1949
	The North Atlantic Treaty Organization (NATO) is formed.
	1957
	The Russians launch Sputnik.
	1966–69
1972	The Chinese Cultural Revolution
Sri Lanka becomes a republic.	
1978	
A presidential system of government is adopted.	
1983	
Liberation Tigers of Tamil Eelam wage war in the north and east.	**1986**
1988	Nuclear power disaster at Chernobyl in Ukraine
Ranasinghe Premadasa is elected president.	**1991**
1993	Break-up of the Soviet Union
President Premadasa is assassinated.	
1994	
Chandrika Kumaratunga is elected president.	**1997**
	Hong Kong is returned to China.
2001	**2001**
Ranil Wickremesinghe becomes prime minister.	World population surpasses 6 billion.

GLOSSARY

bo tree
Ficus religiosa. Prince Siddhartha sat under one in Gaya, India when he attained enlightenment and gave the world the philosophy of Buddhism.

caste
A system categorizing people according to their profession. Tamils and Sinhalese have their own forms of the caste system.

dagoba ("DAH-go-beh")
A Buddhist shrine containing sacred relics of the Buddha or of his disciples.

devale ("DAY-vah-leh")
A Hindu deity, or a Hindu temple containing an image of the god worshiped within.

dhoby ("DHOH-bee")
A person who washes others' clothes and linen.

ganga ("GUNG-gah")
A river.

kovil ("KOH-vil")
A Hindu shrine.

magul kapuwa ("MAH-gool KAH-poo-wah")
A traditional broker of arranged marriages.

namaste ("neh-MEHS-tay")
A gesture of greeting, in which the person bows slightly with the palms of both hands pressed together in front of the chest.

perahera ("PAIR-ah-HAIR-ah")
An elaborate procession of elephants. Major temples have annual *perahera*. Sri Lanka's biggest *perahera* takes place in Kandy.

poya ("POH-yeh")
A Buddhist holy day, the monthly full moon. There are five major ones: Duruthu in January, Vesak in May, Poson in June, Esala in August, and Unduvap in December.

sarama ("SAH-rah-mah")
An ankle-length sarong worn by Sinhalese men.

sari ("SAH-ree")
A large piece of cloth wound around the waist and shoulder. It is worn by Sinhalese and Tamil women, with a blouse and long slip.

sil ("sil")
Observation of the eight or 10 Buddhist precepts. A lay Buddhist keeps five precepts daily.

toddy ("TOD-di")
A beverage with a fair alcoholic content. It is the fermented sap of the talipot or coconut palm inflorescence.

vihare ("VI-haar-eh")
A Buddhist temple.

wewa ("WAY-weh")
An irrigation tank, or manmade lake for collecting and storing water for rice fields.

FURTHER INFORMATION

BOOKS

Barlas, Robert and Nanda Wanasundera. *Culture Shock! Sri Lanka*. Rev. ed. Singapore: Times Books International, 2000.

Bradnock, Robert, Roma Bradnock and Peter Pollard. *Footprint Sri Lanka Handbook*. 3rd ed. New York: McGraw Hill, 2001.

Bullis, Douglas and Wendy Hutton. *The Food of Sri Lanka: Authentic Recipes from the Isle of Gems*. Vermont: Tuttle, 2001.

Campbell, Verity and Christine Niven. *Lonely Planet Sri Lanka*. 8th ed. London: Lonely Planet Publications, 2001.

De Silva, K. M. *A History of Sri Lanka*. Oxford: Oxford University Press, 1981.

Gunaratne, Merril. *Dilemma of an Island*. Colombo: Vijita Yapa, 2001.

Gunesekera, Romesh. *Reef*. New York: Riverhead Books, 1996.

Ondaatje, Michael. *Anil's Ghost*. New York: Knopf, 2000.

Ondaatje, Michael. *Running in the Family*. New York: Vintage International, 1993.

Spittel, R. L. *Savage Sanctuary*. 3rd ed. Colombo: Sooriya, 2000.

Street-Porter, Tim. *Tropical Houses: Living in Nature in Jamaica, Sri Lanka, Java, Mexico, and the Coasts of Mexico and Belize*. New York: Clarkson Potter, 2000.

Wright, E. Bealby. *Insight Guide Sri Lanka*. 4th ed. London: APA, 1999.

WEBSITES

At Sri Lanka: A Comprehensive Travel Portal of Sri Lanka. www.atsrilanka.com

Board of Investment of Sri Lanka. www.boisrilanka.org

Central Intelligence Agency World Factbook (select Sri Lanka from the country list). www.odci.gov/cia/publications/factbook/index.html

Lonely Planet World Guide: Destination Sri Lanka. www.lonelyplanet.com/destinations/indian_subcontinent/sri_lanka/

Official Website of the Government of Sri Lanka. www.priu.gov.lk

Official Website of the Sri Lanka Tourist Board. www.lanka.net/ctb

Sri Lanka: A Country Study. http://memory.loc.gov/frd/cs/lktoc.html

Thakshana e-library. The Sri Lanka Scientific & Technical Information Center's National Science Foundation website. http://thakshana.nsf.ac.lk

The Virtual Library of Sri Lanka. www.lankalibrary.com

The World Bank Group (type "Sri Lanka" in the search box). www.worldbank.org

The World Conservation Union Sri Lanka Country Office. www.iucnsl.org

BIBLIOGRAPHY

Barlas, Robert and Nanda Wanasundera. *Culture Shock! Sri Lanka*. Rev. ed. Singapore: Times Books International, 1999.

Bennett, Gay. *A Family in Sri Lanka*. Minneapolis: Lerner Publications, 1985.

Fernando, Nihal. *Sri Lanka: A Personal Odyssey*. Colombo: Studio Times, 1997.

Sansoni, Dominic and Richard Simon. *Sri Lanka: The Respledent Isle*. Singapore: Times Editions, 1989.

Samarasekara, Ohanapala. *Take a Trip to Sri Lanka*. New York: Franklin Watts, 1987.

Somasekeram, T., et. al. (editors). *Arjuna's Atlas of Sri Lanka*. Dehiwala: Arjuna Consulting, 1997.

Tidball, Tim. *Sri Lanka*. Foreword by Arthur C. Clarke. Colombo: Foremost, 1991.

APA Guide: Sri Lanka. Hong Kong: APA, 1991.

Sri Lanka. New York: Chelsea House, 1988.

Sri Lanka in Pictures. Minneapolis: Lerner Publications, 1989.

INDEX